Little Red Book
of
Euphemisms

By the same author

Little Red Book Series

Little Red Book of Slang-Chat Room Slang	Little Red Book of Synonyms
Little Red Book of English Vocabulary Today	Little Red Book of Antonyms
	Little Red Book of Common Errors
Little Red Book of Grammar Made Easy	Little Red Book of Letter Writing
	Little Red Book of Essay Writing
Little Red Book of English Proverbs	Little Red Book of Word Fact
Little Red Book of Prepositions	Little Red Book of Spelling
Little Red Book of Idioms and Phrases	Little Red Book of Language Checklist
Little Red Book of Effective Speaking Skills	Little Red Book of Perfect Written English
Little Red Book of Phrasal Verbs	Little Red Book of Punctuation
Little Red Book of Euphemisms	Little Red Book of Reading and Listening
Little Red Book of Word Power	
Little Red Book of Modern Writing Skills	Little Red Book of A Child's First Dictionary

A2Z Book Series

A2Z Quiz Book	A2Z Book of Word Origins

Others

The Book of Fun Facts	The Book of Motivation
The Book of More Fun Facts	Read Write Right: Common Errors in English
The Book of Firsts and Lasts	
The Book of Virtues	The Students' Companion
World Facts Finder	

Fun Facts: Science	Fun with Maths
Fun Facts: Animals	Fun with Numbers
Fun Facts: India	Fun with Puzzles
Fun Facts: Nature	Fun with Riddles

Little Red Book *of* Euphemisms

Terry O'Brien

RUPA

Published by
Rupa Publications India Pvt. Ltd 2011
7/16, Ansari Road, Daryaganj
New Delhi 110002

Sales centres:
Bengaluru Chennai
Hyderabad Jaipur Kathmandu
Kolkata Mumbai Prayagraj

Copyright © Terry O' Brien 2011

The views and opinions expressed in this book are the
author's own and the facts are as reported by him which
have been verified to the extent possible, and the publishers
are not in any way liable for the same.

All rights reserved.
No part of this publication may be reproduced, transmitted,
or stored in a retrieval system, in any form or by any means,
electronic, mechanical, photocopying, recording or otherwise,
without the prior permission of the publisher.

P-ISBN: 978-81-291-1806-6
E-ISBN: 978-93-5333-904-3

Tenth impression 2025

13 12 11 10

The moral right of the author has been asserted.

Typeset by Innovative Processors, New Delhi

Printed in India

This book is sold subject to the condition that it shall not, by way of
trade or otherwise, be lent, resold, hired out, or otherwise circulated,
without the publisher's prior consent, in any form of binding or cover
other than that in which it is published.

*I dedicate this book to late Prof. A.P. O'Brien,
my father, friend, guide and mentor, who
inspired me to the canon of excellence:
re-imagining what's essential*

PREFACE

A **euphemism** (from the Greek words **eu** - *well* and **pheme** - *speak*) is a word or expression that is used when people want to find a polite or less direct way of talking about difficult or embarrassing topics like death or the bodily functions. If the sick old dog had to be killed, they would soften the pain by saying: **We had Jimmy put to sleep**. Many people prefer to call someone **plain** than ugly, or **cuddly** rather than fat. Thus euphemisms are an important part of every language. English has an ever-growing number of them.

When your friend needs to use the toilet your American friend asks where is the **bathroom** (or restroom, or comfort station or **wash room**); an Englishman may most likely ask for **'the geography of the house"** or may want to **see a man about a dog**. We might have learned, for example, that **in the family way** is a euphemism for pregnant: **Congratulations! I hear your wife is in the family way**

Schools are full of euphemisms. At school, for example, the special lessons given to students who are having difficulties in their school subjects are called **Study Center** (in the middle school) and **Academic Workshop** (in the high school). Teachers rightly do not want to offend students or parents by being too blunt or direct, and usually choose a softer word or expression to convey the same message. For this reason, school reports often contain euphemisms such as: **He is not working to his full potential** or **He has a rather relaxed attitude to his work** (= he is lazy), **She**

is unable to concentrate in class (= she is disruptive), **He has strong opinions about everything and is not afraid to voice them** (= he is loud and arrogant).

Typical of many recently-coined euphemisms are the words and expressions that try to avoid giving offence to various minority groups or unfortunate individuals. People who have severe learning difficulties are sometimes called **intellectually-challenged**, and those with a physical handicap are referred to as **differently-abled**. Poor people are called **needy**, **under-privileged**; **disadvantaged** or **economically deprived**. Poor countries have in turn been called **underdeveloped, developing, emergent, Third World** - all in an effort to retain the meaning without causing offence. A **senior citizen** is an old person; **collateral damage** are civilians killed in bombing attacks on a city; **a law-enforcement officer** a policeman; **pro-choice** describes a person who is a supporter of a woman's right to have an abortion (opponents of abortion call themselves **pro-life**); **white meat** - the meat that comes from the breast of a chicken; **adult movie** - pornographic movie; **economical with the truth** is someone who is economical with the truth is actually is a liar; **tired and emotional** means drunk; **person with a visual impairment** refers to a blind person; a **substance abuser** is a drug addict; **downsizing** means reducing the size and wages bill of a company by sacking employees. **Where can I wash my hands?** Would be a question meaning - Where is the toilet? In the US they have their set of unique euphemisms: **A vertically challenged** is used to describe a short person!

Here comes the *Little Red Book of Euphemisms*. Let us get politically correct!

Happy reading
Terry O'Brien

A2Z Euphemisms: Glossary

A

Ableism	Insensitivity towards lame or injured people.
Ablutions	Lavatories - *originally, the rite of cleaning, from which washing and then the place where you wash*
Above your ceiling	Promoted to a level beyond your abilities
Absent parent	A parent who does not live with his or her infant child or children usually, the father, who is not just away on a business trip
Abuse	The use of a person or object for a taboo or illegal purpose
Accost	To approach a stranger with a taboo request or suggestion
Accumulate	(of securities) do not sell: *Jargon of the financial analyst whose job is to promote activity among investors rather than pass them bad news*
Acknowledgement	The payment of bribe
Activist	A political zealot. *No longer merely a supporter of the philosophy of activism but someone willing to break the law in pursuit of strongly held beliefs*

Administrative	Detention, imprisonment without trial
Administrative leave	Suspension from duty for alleged malpractice
Advantaged	Rich
Adverse event (an)	A death
Aerated	Drunk - *Literally, describing a liquid charged with gas, rather than a body charged with liquid. Aerated, of a person, may also mean angry or agitated*
Affair	An ongoing relationship with other than your regular sexual partner
Afflicted	Subject to physical or mental illness or abnormality
Affordable	Cheap - *used to describe household equipment or small newly built houses*
Afloat	Drunk
After-shave	A perfume used by males
Afterlife	Death
Afterthought	A child born in wedlock following an unplanned conception
Aggressive	Recklessly optimistic or dishonest
Aid	A gift from a rich to a poor country
Airport novel	A book written for a person who does not read regularly
All night man	A dealer in corpses

Alley Cat	A prostitute
Allow your name to go forward	To seek election to a public office
Alter the demographics	To practice genocide
Alternative	Differing from existing social arrangement, practicality, or convention
Another state (in a)	Dead
Anorak	An enthusiast for an intellectual pastime
Answer the call	To die
Answer the call	To go to the lavatory
Anti-social	Criminal or offensive
Apple-polish	To seek favour or advancement by flattery
Appropriate	To steal
Ardent spirits	Spirituous intoxicants
Arm candy	A good-looking female companion
Armed struggle (the)	Terrorism
Army form blank	Lavatory paper
Arrange	To do something underhand, shameful, or taboo
Ask for your papers	To resign from employment

Associate with	To meet in an illegal or taboo capacity
At government	Expense in prison
At it	Engaged in a taboo activity
At rest	Dead
At your last	About to die
Attention deficit disorder	Idleness, stupidity or indiscipline
Aunt	A promiscuous woman or prostitute
Available	Involuntarily unemployed
Axe	To kill after judicial process
Axe	To dismiss summarily from employment
Aztec two step (the)	Diarrhoea

B

BO	The smell of stale sweat
Baby-snatcher	A person with a much younger regular sexual partner
Bacchanalian	Drunken
Backdoor	Involving bribery or impropriety
Back teeth floating	Having drunk too much alcohol and wishing to go to the washroom
Backhander	A bribe
Backward	Very stupid
Backward	Poor or uncivilized
Bad-mouth	To denigrate

Badge bandit	A highway police officer
Bagged	Drunk
Bait and switch	Obtaining investment funds by deceit
Bake	To kill
Balance of mind disturbed	Temporarily insane
Bamboo curtain	The censorship and other restrictions in China to limit knowledge of and contracts with foreigners
Bamboozled	Drunk
Banana	Do not allow any development here The acronym of *Build absolutely Nothing Anywhere Near Anyone*; Nimby – *Not in My Backyard*
Bananas	Mentally disturbed: *The fruit is favored by monkeys. The phrase is often used to refer to mild hysteria*
Bandwagon	A cause or chance for profit which attracts opportunists
Basement	A lavatory
Basket case	A person, institution, or society incapable of self-reliance
Bathroom	A lavatory
Bats in the belfry	Mental abnormality
Battered	Drunk
Battle fatigue	The inability to continue fighting
Bay window	A fat person's stomach

Be excused	To go to the lavatory
Beat the gong	To smoke opium
Bed	Childbirth
Bedwetting	Involuntarily wetting in a bed
Behind the eight ball	In serious difficulty: *from a potentially losing position in the game of pool*
Bell Money	A levy on a bridegroom at a wedding
Belly up	Bankrupt
Below medium height	Short
Below stairs	Employed as a domestic servant
Below the salt	Socially inferior
Belt	A taboo article or activity
Bench	To cause to withdraw from active participation
Bend	To drink intoxicants to excess
Bend sinister	An imputation of illegitimacy
Bend the rules	To act illegally
Benders	The legs
Bestseller	A book of which the first impression is not remaindered
Bet the farm	To make a risky decision or investment
Beyond the blanket	Conceived outside marriage
Big-boned	Fat
Big D (the)	Death

Billingsgate	Foul language
Bimbo	A sexually complaisant female
Bin	An institution for the insane
Binge	To go on a drunken carouse
Bint	A prostitute
Biological clock	Referring to the increasing difficulty of women conceiving due to ageing
Bird	A young female companion
Bird dog	Someone working for a criminal
Birth control	The prevention of conception.
Birthday suit (your)	Nakedness
Bit missing (a)	Of low intelligence
Bite the bullet	To take a difficult or costly decision
Bite the dust	To die
Black	Associated with illegality
Black bag (associated with)	An illicit inquiry: *usually relating to telephone tapping or the robbery of documents*
Black job	A funeral
Back lad	The devil
Black smoke	Opium
Blackmail	Extortion by threats
Bladdered	Drunk
Blast	A mild oath
Bleed	To extort money from on a regular basis

Bleeding heart	A person who ostentatiously expresses concern about or seeks to relieve the suffering of others
Blitzed	Drunk
Block out	To kill
Blockbuster	A novel which is expected to sell well
Blood money	Extortion
Blooming	A mild oath
Blot (out)	To kill
Blow away	To kill
Blue-eyed boy	Someone favoured by his superiors
Blue hair	An old woman
Blue ribbon	Teetotal
Blue ruin	Gin
Boat people	Political or economic refugees fleeing a country by sea
Bobby	A policeman
Boiled	Drunk
Bolt	Suddenly leave home, desert a spouse, or bilk your creditors
Booby	A mentally ill person: *literally, a fool. A booby hatch or hutch is an institution for the insane*
Book	A sentence in prison
Bookmaker	A person who accepts bets for a living
Boom-passenger	A convict sentenced to transportation

Boost	To steal
Boot money	A wrongful payment to an amateur in sport
Bootleg	Smuggled or stolen: *originally, it referred to intoxicants, supposedly from the bottles concealed on the legs when transporting supplies illegally to American Indians*
Boston marriage	Two women sharing a home
Both oars in the water	Mentally normal
Bottle blond(e)	A woman with hair dyed yellow
Bottle club	An unlicensed establishment where alcohol is drunk
Bottom fishing	Buying a security whose price has fallen
Box	A coffin
Brace	To kill: *literally, to fasten tightly or strengthen*
Bracer	A spirituous intoxicant
Brahms	Drunk
Branch water	Which is offered from a bottle
Brass (the)	Senior management
Brasser	A prostitute
Break your elbow	To give birth to a child outside marriage
Breathe your last	To die

Little Red Book of Euphemisms

Brew	To burn
Brew (a)	Beer
Brick short of a load (a)	Of low intelligence
Brief	To disclose information which is misleading or incomplete
Bring down	To kill by shooting
Broken home	A family with young children whose parents have parted
Bromide job	A superficial excuse or explanation
Brown envelope	A bribe
Brown-nose	To flatter
Brown tea	An intoxicant
Browse	To steal and consume food within a store
Bucket shop	An insubstantial vendor of overvalued securities or cut-price services
Bug-eyed	Drunk: *referring to the protrusion of the eyeballs*
Bughouse	Mentally unbalanced: *from the insects figuratively buzzing round in the head*
Bun on (a)	Drunkenness
Bun-puncher	A person who never drinks intoxicants
Bunch of fives	A fist used as a weapon
Bung	A bribe

Burn with a (low) blue flame	To be very drunk: *the imagery is from a dying fire, about to go out*
Burst	To have an urgent need to urinate
Bush-house	A house selling intoxicants
Bush marriage	A marriage performed without due ceremony: *in a remote place the registrar or priest may not be available*
Bust a string	To become mentally unbalanced: *alluding to tennis rather than playing a fiddle*
Button (man)	A professional killer: *presumably one presses him for action*
Buzz on (a)	Drunk or under the influence of narcotics: *from the ringing in the ears or general air of excitement*
By mutual consent	Without litigation: *corporate speak when a senior manager is dismissed and damages are agreed between the parties*
By yourself	Mad: *in a world of your own!*

C

Cabbage	To steal
California widow	A deserted wife
Call off all bets	To die

Calorie counter	A fat person: *Advertising jargon, suggesting that the physical condition is not due to gluttony, the lack of exercise*
Camel	A smuggler of illegal narcotics
Cameo	A minor screen appearance by a well-known performer
Campaign wife	A mistress
Canned goods	A virgin
Cannon	A pickpocket
Canteen medal	An exposed trouser fly button
Cardiac incident	A malfunction of the heart
Career change	Dismissal from employment
Careful	Stingy
Carousel	A fraud involving tax repayment
Carpet bombing	Delivering to recipients multiple unsolicited advertising circulars
Carpetbagger	A seeker of short-term gain: *originally, an absconding American banker*
Carry	To be pregnant (with)
Carry	A card to be a member of the Communist party
Carry off	To cause the death of: *It is used of dying from an epidemic or sudden illness*
Carry the can	To receive undeserved punishment while the culprit goes free

Carsey	A lavatory
Cash flow problem	An insolvency
Cash in hand	Payment for goods or services avoiding taxation
Cash in your checks	To die
Casual	An institution which housed the destitute
Catch	A rich marriageable adult
Catch a cold	To have a trouser zip undone
Catch a packet	To be killed or severally wounded
Catch fish with a silver hook	To pretend to have caught fish which you have bought
Category killer	A cut-price store in a shopping precinct
Cease to be	To die
Celebrate	To drink intoxicants to excess
Celebrity	A person employed as an entertainer
Certifiable	Mentally unstable but still at liberty
Chair (the)	Judicial death by electrocution
Chair-days	Old age
Chalk-board	A blackboard
Change	To replace by a clean one: *a soiled napkin on a baby*
Change your bulbs	To become subject to mental abnormality

Change your jacket	To desert an old allegiance
Chapel of ease	A mortuary
Charlie	A substitute word for a taboo subject or expression
Charlie Ronce	A pimp
Charm	To effect a magical cure
Chase the dragon	To smoke a narcotic
Cheat the starter	To conceive a child before marriage
Check into Crowbar Hotel	*American to send to prison*
Cheese eater	A cheat
Cheesecake	An erotic picture of a female
Cherry-pick	Fraudulently to select bargain
Chew a gun	To kill yourself
Chi-chi	Of mixed white and Indian ancestry: *a derogatory use. It means dirty in Hindi*
Chicago typewriter	A sub-machine gun: *a combination of the noise of the machine and the city's reputation for lawlessness*
Chicken	Cowardly
Child of sin	An illegitimate child
Child of Venus	A prostitute
China white	Heroin: *the colour, the origin, and the porcelain*

Chinese book-keeping	False accounting
Chinese copy	A production model stolen from another's design
Chinese-fire-drill (a)	Pandemonium
Chinese paper	A security of doubtful value: *commercial jargon*
Chinese parliament a	Disorganized discussion group
Chinese (three-point) landing	A crash on the runway
Chinese tobacco	Opium
Chinese wall	The pretence that price-sensitive information will not be used by an advisor or his associates to their own advantage
Chinese whisper	An unsubstantiated rumour
Chirp	to be an informer to the police
Chisel	To steal or cheat
Chokey	A prison
Chop	To kill
Chop (the)	Sudden dismissal from employment
Chota peg	A spirituous intoxicant: *Chota is small in Hindi, although the measure may not be; a burra peg is an even larger measure of spirits*

Little Red Book of Euphemisms

Chubby	Fat
Chuck (the)	Peremptory dismissal from employment, school or courtship
Chuck seven	To die
Chuck up	To vomit
Churn	To deal unnecessarily in client's securities in order to generate commission
Circular	File a waste paper basket
Claim responsibility for	To admit to
Claret	Blood: *boxing jargon, of blood from the nose*
Clean	House to remove incriminating evidence
Clean up	To bring the proceeds of vice into open circulation
Clean up	Illegally to destroy evidence
Cleanse	To free from enemy occupation or sympathizers
Cleavage	The division between a woman's breasts
Clink off	To die: *to depart*
Clip	To swindle or rob
Clip his wick	To kill: *Like putting out a candle by cutting the wick below where it was burning*
Cloakroom	A lavatory
Clobbered	Drunk

Little Red Book of Euphemisms 17

Clock	Fraudulently to alter the reading of a milometer
Clock-watcher	A disinterested employee
Cloot	The devil
Close	Stingy
Close its doors	To fail
Close stool	A portable lavatory
Closet	A lavatory
Clothes horse	An expensively dressed woman
Clunk	A corpse
Cock the little finger	To be addicted to alcohol: *the manner in which some hold a cup*
Cocktail	A mixture of alcohol or illegal narcotics
Coco made	A Second World War military use, sometimes a *cocoa*
Coffee-housing	Cheating at cards: *refers to the behaviour of whist players in 18th century London coffee houses*
Coke	Cocaine ingested illegally: *a shortened form, without reference to the carbonated beverage*
A cookie	An addict: *thereby becoming coked*
Cold	Dead
Cold Feet	Cowardice or fear
Cold turkey	The effect of sudden and sustained deprivation of narcotics

Cold-water man	Person who drinks no alcohol
Collaborator	A traitor
Collaborator	A ghost writer: *the labour is mostly done by the ghost*
Collar	To steal
Collateral damage	Killing or wounding civilians by mistake: *literally, damage running alongside*
Colombian gold	High quality marijuana
Colony	A distant territory ruled by expatriates
Colour	Relating to racial descent
Colour-tinted	Dyed
Colourful	Amoral or defying convention: *A catch-all word for journalists wary of defamation*
Comb	Out to massacre
Combat fatigue	An unwillingness or inability to continue fighting
Combat ineffective	Died, seriously ill, or badly wounded
Come home	Feet first to be killed: *Corpse are usually carried that way, although the opposite happens with coffin*
Come into the public domain	To cease being a secret

Come through	To act under duress
Come to your resting place	To die
Come up with the rations	To be awarded as a matter of routine
Comfort women	Japanese army prostitutes
Commercial sex worker	A prostitute
Commission	A bribe
Commit a nuisance	To urinate in public: *usually of a male, where commit meant perform and nuisance is legal jargon for an offensive act*
Committee (the)	An instrument of state repression
Commode	A portable lavatory
Common house	A lavatory
Community of wives	Polyandry
Company (the)	Organization for espionage and foreign subversion
Complimentary	Included in the price
Comprehension	The ability to read
Compromise	To expose to embarrassment or danger
Con	To trick

Concentration camp	A place for arbitrary imprisonment of political and other opponents
Concert party	The concerted buying of shares in a company using different names
Concession	A reduction in an inflated demand
Concessional	Free or subsidized
Concoct	To falsify
Concrete shoes (in)	Murdered and hidden: *A more accurate description of cement shoes, and also as concrete boots or overcoat*
Condition	An illness
Conduct disorder	Habitual disobedience, selfishness, and incivility
Confederation	A pressure group
Conference (in)	Unwilling to see or talk to callers
Confident pricing	Charging more for the same product
Confinement	The period of childbirth
Confused	Drunk: *It certainly can take one that way*
Conk (out)	To die
Consumption	Pulmonary tuberculosis
Contract	A promise of payment to murder (someone)
Controversial	Politically damaging
Convenience	A lavatory for public use
Conventional	Not involving nuclear or germ warfare

Cook	To kill
Cook	Fraudulently to alter
Cookie	A promiscuous female
Cooler	A prison
Cooperate	To assist another through fear or duress
Cop	A policeman
Cop an elephant's	To become intoxicated
Cop out	Plead guilty to a minor offence in return for the prosecution dropping a more serious charge
Copper	A policeman: *from the metal buttons on their 19th century uniforms, but cop offers an alternative etymology*
Co-respondent	A male accused at law of having cuckolded another
Corked	Drunk
Corn	Low-grade whisky
Corn-fed	Plump
Corner	To establish a monopoly in an essential product
Corporate	Entertainment bribery: *when customers are given treats at the firm's expenses*
Corporate recovery	The management or winding-up of insolvent companies
Correction	A serious fall (in value)

Corridor creeping	Extramarital copulation
Costume wedding	The marriage of a pregnant bride
Couch potato	A person who habitually spends leisure time watching television
Counter-insurgency	Waging war in another country
Country sports	Killing wild animals for pleasure
Courtesy	Included in the price
Crack	To rob
Crack	To hit or kill
Crack a bottle	To drink wine
Cradle-snatcher	An older person marrying one much younger
Crash	To return to normality after taking an illegal narcotic
Crease	To kill by violence
Credibility gap	The extent to which you are thought to be lying
Creep-joint	A brothel
Criminal conversation	Adultery
Criminal operation	An illegal abortion
Crinkly	Old or an old person
Croak	To die

Crocked	Drunk
Cross the floor	To change political allegiance
Cross the Styx	To die
Cross your palm	To bribe
Crumbly	An old person
Crystal	Cocaine
Cuban heels	Thick soles and heels on footwear to enhance height
Cull	To kill
Cult	Appealing only to a minority
Cultural	Having characteristics differing from the norm
Cumshaw	A bribe
Currency adjustment	A devaluation
Curry colonel	A staff officer in the Indian Navy
Curtains	Death
Custody suite	A prison cell
Cut	Drunk
Cut-and-paste job	A report sloppily prepared from various sources
Cut numbers	To make employee redundant
Cut out	To deprive (someone) of something valuable
Cut the painter	To die

D

D & C	The abortion of a foetus
DCM	A notice of dismissal from employment
Daily	A non-resident domestic servant
Daisy chain	A gathering or association to carry out a taboo activity
Damp	An alcoholic drink
Dark man	The devil
Dark meat	The flesh of poultry other than the breast
Dark moon	A wife's secret savings
Darn	A mild oath
Dash	To adulterate a drink
Date	A heterosexual companion
Davy Jones's locker	A grave at sea
Day of action	A politically motivated strike
Daylight	Associated with killing by shooting
Dead meat	A human corpse
Dead soldier	An empty bottle of wine or spirits
Deal from the bottom of the deck	To lie or cheat
Debt of honour	Unpaid money lost at gambling
Decadent	Not conforming to accepted tastes
Decommission	Wearing clothes which hide any suggestion of nakedness

Decks awash	Drunk
Decommission	To dismiss an employee
Decrease in footfall (a)	Less customers
Deep freeze	A prison
Defecate	Defecation
Defence	Aggression
Defensive victory	A defeat
Delhi belly	Diarrhoea
Delinquency	A bad debt
Demands of nature	Urination and defecation
Demise	A death
Demonstration	A mass assembly to protest about a specific issue
Depart (this life)	To die
Deprived	Poor
Derailed	Mad
Derbyshire neck	A goiter
Designer	More expensive
Destroy	To kill
Dickens	The devil
Diddle	To urinate
Destroy	To kill

Die queer	To kill yourself
Die with your knees bent	To be killed in an electric chair
Diet of worms	A corpse
Dip	To steal
Diplomatic	Pretended to avoid an obligation
Direct mail	Unsolicited enquiries sent by post
Directional selling	Promoting the product of an associated company without disclosing the financial link
Disco biscuit	An ecstasy tablet
Discrimination	Selective and unfair treatment of others
Disengage	To retreat
Dish	A sexually attractive woman
Disinfection	Mass killing
Disinvestment	The disposal of shares etc. as a political gesture
Dismal trade	The arranging of funerals for payment
Disorderly house	A brothel
Dispatch	To kill
Dispose	Of to kill
Dispute	A strike
Dissolution	Death
Distressed	Mentally ill
Disturbed	Mentally abnormal

Dive	A place for the sale and drinking of intoxicants
Divert	To steal
Do a bunk	To urinate
Do a number (of a criminal)	To give information to the police
Do away with	To kill
Do-gooder	A self-righteous person who forces his concerns on others
Do-lally-tap	Mad
Do the right thing	To marry a woman you have impregnated
Doctor to	Change through deception
Doe	Prostitute
Dog and pony show	A bogus exhibition or insincere conduct calculated to deceive
Dole	A payment by the state to the involuntarily unemployed
Doll	A sexually attractive female
Dollar shop	A store which will not sell in the local currency
Dolly	A mistress
Domestic	A servant in the home
Don Juan	A male philanderer
Donation	A bribe
Doorstep	To abandon a baby
Dope	A narcotic

Dose of P45 medicine	The summary dismissal of employees
Double dipper	A person in receipt of bribery or a second source of income
Double entry	Dishonest
Double time	Affair outside marriage
Douceur	A bribe
Dove	An appeaser or pacifist
Down population	The compulsory dismissal of employees
Down's syndrome	A congenital disorder due to a chromosome deficiency
Downs	Depressant narcotics
Downsize	To dismiss employee
Downstairs	The house servants
Doxy	A prostitute
Drag	The clothing of the other sex worn by a homosexual
Dragon (the)	Habitual illegal use of narcotics
Draw a blank	To be very drunk
Draw water	To have power or influence
Dress for sale	A prostitute
Drip gas	Stolen petroleum
Drop anchor	Fraudulently to cause a horse to run slowly in a race
Drown the miller	To be made bankrupt

Drown your sorrow	To drink intoxicants to excess
Drumstick	The thigh of a cooked bird
Dry	Prohibiting or not offering the sale of intoxicants
Dry	To forget your lines
Dummy	A stupid person
Dunny	A lavatory
Dutch	*Appears in many offensive and often euphemistic expressions dating from the 17th century antagonism between England and the Low Countries*
Dutch	Unpopular
Dutch (do the)	To kill yourself
Dutch auction	An auction in which the auctioneer drops the price until a buyer makes a bid
Dutch bargain	An unfair or unprofitable deal
Dutch cheer	A drink of spirits: *the Dutch are supposed to be gloomy when sober*
Dutch clock	A bed pan: *from the shape and contents*
Dutch comfort	An assumption that things cannot get worse
Dutch consolation	An assurance that, although things are bad, they could have been worse
Dutch Course	Bravery induced by intoxicants, implying a Dutchman is a coward when he is sober

Dutch dinner	A meal to which you are invited but have to pay
Dutch feast	An occasion where the host becomes drunk while his guests are still sober
Dutch headache	A hangover
Dutch reckoning	An inflated bill without details
Dutch roll	Combined yaw and roll in an aircraft which behaves with the gait of a drunken sailor
Dutch Treat	An entertainment or a meal to which you are invited but where you have to pay for yourself
Dutch uncle	Someone who reproves you sharply or gives you solemn advice, unlike the supposed geniality of real uncles
Dutch widow	A prostitute
Dutch wife	A bolster
Dutchman	A stupid person
Duty not paid	Smuggled
Duvet day	An unjustified absence from work tolerated by an employer

E

Ear	A clandestine microphone
Early bath	Dismissal from a team game
Early release	Dismissal from employment

Little Red Book of Euphemisms 31

Earn a passport	To be rewarded as an assassin
Earth closet	A non-flush lavatory
Earthy	Vulgar
Easy terms	Hire purchase
Easy way out (the)	Suicide
Eat a gun	To commit suicide with a firearm
Eat-in kitchen	A kitchen incorporating a dining area
Eat porridge	To be in prison
Eat stale dog	To take a deserved reprimand
Eat the Bible	American to perjure yourself
Eating disorder	Anorexia nervosa or bulimia
Eccentric	Severally ill mentally
Economical with the truth	Lying
Economically disadvantaged	Poor
Economically inactive	Unemployed
Economy	Cheap
Ecstasy	An illegal stimulant
Edged	Slightly drunk
Efficiency	A single-roomed apartment
Effing	An oath
Elbow-bending	Drinking intoxicants

Eliminate	To kill
Embalmed	Very drunk
Embroidery	Exaggeration or lying
Emergency	A political suspension of civil rights
Emergent	Poor and uncivilized
Empty a saddle	To kill someone
Empty nesters	A childless couple
Energy release	An accidental release of radioactive material
Entanglement	An embarrassing or clandestine association
Entitlement	State payment to the poor
Eternal life	Death
Evasion	A lie
Eve	A female
Everlasting life	Death
Everlasting staircase	A treadmill
Excess	To make a charge additional to the published tariff
Executive measure	A political murder
Exemplary punishment	Death by hanging
Expand your balance sheet	To borrow more
Expectant	Pregnant

Expedient demise	An unlawful killing by a government agency
Expended	Killed
Experienced	Not new
Expire	To die
Expletive deleted	An obscenity
Expose	To leave in the open to die
Extinguish	To kill
Extrajudicial killing	State-sponsored assassination
Extramarital excursion	A sexual relationship outside marriage
Eye-candy	A nubile young woman
Eye-opener	An intoxicant or stimulant taken on waking

F

Face your maker	To be mortally ill
Facilitation payment	To bribe
Facility	A lavatory
Facility	An agreement to lend money by a bank
Fact-finding	Taking a holiday at public expense
Fade away	To die

Fail to win	To lose
Fair trader	A smuggler
Fairly	A homosexual
Fall asleep	To die
Fall off the back of a lorry	To be stolen
Fall out of bed	To fail commercially or in a plea
Fallen woman	A promiscuous female
Falling sickness (the)	Epilepsy
Family	The Mafia
Family planning	Contraception
Fan club	People who clandestinely copy the actions of another
Fancy	To lust after
Fanny	The buttocks
Fanny Adams	Nothing
Far from staunch	Cowardly
Far gone	Drunk
Fat cat	A person who exploits a senior appointment for personal gain
Fat finger	An erroneous commercial transaction
Father of lie	The devil
Fatigue mental	Illness
Feather-bed	To grant excessive indulgence towards

Feather your nest	To provide for yourself at the expense of others
Federal camp	A prison
Fee note	A request for payment
Feed the fishes	To be seasick
Feed the meter	Illegally to extend a period of parking
Feel a collar	To arrest someone
Fiddle	To steal by cheating
Field associate	A police officer charged with detecting police corruption
Fifth column	Traitors within your ranks
Fifty cards in the pack	Of low intelligence
File thirteen	A wastepaper basket
Fill full of holes	To kill by shooting
Filly	A young woman viewed sexual by a male
Financial service	Money-lending
Financial excluded	Unable to open a bank account
Find a tree	To urinate
Find Cook County	To engage in electoral fraud
Fireman	A motorist exceeding the speed limit
Firewater	Whisky

First world	Rich
Fisherman's tale	A lie or exaggeration
Fishing fleet	Marriageable girls
Fishmonger's daughter	A prostitute
Fistful	A prison sentence of five years
Fit up	To incriminate falsely
Five-fingered discount	Shop lifting
Flapper	A young woman who flouts convention
Flat-backer	A prostitute
Flavoured	Scandalous or obscene
Fleece	To defraud
Fleshpot	A brothel
Flexible	Unprincipled
Fling	An extramarital sexual relationship
Float paper	To issue cheques or other securities unsecured by bank deposits or assets
Fly a flag	To have a trouser zip inadvertently undone
Fly a kite	To tender to a worthless negotiable instrument
Fly a kite	To write a begging letter
Fly-by-night	An absconding debtor

Fly the blue pigeon	To steal lead
Fly the yellow flag	To have contagious fever abroad
Flyblow	An illegitimate child
Flyer	An unsolicited advertising leaflet
Flying handicap	Diarrhoea
Flying squad	A police detachment organized for rapid deployment
Foggy	Drunk
Fold back	To retreat
Fondle	A caress sexually
Food for worms	Dead
Footless	Drunk
For the birds	Mentally unbalanced
For your convenience	Provided ostensibly as a special service
Forage	To steal
Forty-four	A prostitute
Foul play	Murder
Four-letter man	An unpleasant person
Four-letter word	An obscenity
Fourth	A lavatory

Foxed	Drunk
Foxtrot Oscar	A vulgar rebuttal
Fraternal assistance	An invasion
Freak a devotee	Of any taboo or unconventional activity
Free	Included in the price
Free trade	Smuggling
Free world	Those countries not under Communist control
Freedom fighters	Rebels
Freeze on to	To steal
Freezer	A prison
French	*is used by the English of anything which they consider bogus, overrated, illegal, immoral, or otherwise undesirable, reflecting the mutual distrust between the countries which was not lessened by the events between 1940 and 1945*
French	To include in oral sex
French	An excuse for swearing
French ache	Syphilis
French article	Smuggled brandy
French drive	A miscued shot at cricket
French leave	Unauthorized absence
French novel	A salacious book

French pigeon	A pheasant shot out of season
French prints	Pornographic picture
French renovating pills	Substance to induce abortion of a healthy foetus
Freshen up	Drunk
Fried	Drunk
Friendly	Lacking accord or sympathy
Fringe	Unconventional, insubstantial, or fraudulent
Front-running	Dealing illegally as an insider
Frosting	Stealing motor cars
Fruit machine	A mechanical gambling device
Fry	To die
Fuddled	Drunk
Fudge	To attempt to deceive
Full figure (a)	Obesity
Full in the belly	Pregnant
Funny money	Cash which cannot be spent openly
Furry thing	A rabbit
Fuzz	The police

G

Gaffe	An embarrassing statement of unpalatable truth
Gallant	A women's extramarital sexual partner
Game	Wild animals killed primarily for human amusement

Gamester	A gambler
Gander-mooner	A husband copulating outside marriage
Gap year	A long period of inactivity between secondary and tertiary education
Gardening leave	Suspension from office on full pay
Gathered to God	Dead
Gear	Anything which is the subject of secrecy or taboo
Generously built (of a woman)	Fat
Gentleman friend	Woman's sexual partner to whom she is not married
Gentleman	A lavatory exclusively for male use
Gentry	The fairies
Geography	The location of a lavatory
Get a result	Not to lose
Get along	To grow old
Get on your bike	To be dismissed from employment
Get out the onion	To weep in order to gain sympathy
Get the needle	To be judicially killed
Get the shaft	To receive harsh, precipitate, or unfair treatment

Get the shorts	To be insolvent
Get your feet under the table	To achieve a comfortable and stable domestic situation
Ghost	A writer whose work is published under another's name
Gild	To tell a lie about
Ginger	Homosexual
Gippy tummy	Diarrhoea
Girls' (room)	A lavatory for exclusively female use
Give a P45	British to dismiss peremptorily from employment
Give (someone)	The air to dismiss from employment
Give time to other commitments	To be peremptorily dismissed from employment
Give up the ghost	To die
Give your life	To be killed fighting in a war
Given new responsibilities	Demoted
Glasgow kiss	A headbutt
Glass ceiling	A level above which certain categories of people are unlikely to be promoted
Glass house	An army prison
Glove money	A bribe
Glow	To sweat
Go down	To go to prison

Go down the tube(s)	To fail
Go for your tea	To be murdered
Go on the box	To be absent from work through illness
Go over	To defect
Go slow	A deliberate failure to complete the work allocated
Go south	To lose value or fail
Go to heaven in a string	To be hanged
Go to the wall	To fail or be destroyed
Go up the river	To be sentenced to jail
Go walkabout	To be stolen
God's child	An idiot
God's own medicine	A narcotic or hallucinogen
God's waiting room	A retirement institution for geriatrics
Gold-digger	A woman who consorts with a man because he is rich
Gold plating	Excessive bureaucratic regulation
Gold shot	Bribes

Golden	Large or excessive • *golden goodbye or handshake:* a payment in lieu of damages when an employee is dismissed before the expiry of a contract • *golden hello:* to induce someone to join an employer and perhaps matching any accrued benefits from the previous jobs • *golden handcuffs:* to discourage an employee from leaving to join a competitor • *golden parachute*: to ensure a soft landing in the case of dismissal or a takeover, and less often, but with more width • *golden retriever*: to induce a former employee to return
Golden boy	Someone unfairly favoured or marked for undue promotion
Goner	A person about to die or who has just died
Good lunch (a)	A meal at which excessive alcohol is drunk
Goof	A habitual user of illegal narcotics
Gooseberry	The devil
Gooseberry bush	The place where new boy babies are found
Governmental relations	Bribery or coercion

Grab	To steal
Graft	Bribery
Granny farming	A form of vote rigging: *registering votes by proxy on behalf of muddled and deceived geriatrics*
Grass	Marijuana
Grass widow	A woman of marriageable age separated for an extended period for her husband
Grassed down	Died
Gravy train (the)	A situation in which supplemental benefits are received gratuitously
Graze	To steal and eat food in a supermarket
Grease	To bribe
Greek gift	A present with dire consequences
Green gown	An indication of unchastity in an unmarried woman
Greenmailer	A corporate raider who seeks to get paid to go away
Greying	Growing old
Greymail	A threat to tell state secrets if prosecuted
Groceries	Sundries; intoxicants
Groggy	Drunk
Gross height excursion	A dangerous and unplanned loss of aircraft height
Growth	A cancerous growth

Grunter	A pig
Guest worker	An alien employed without the right of permanent residence
Gumshoe	An investigator in plain clothes
Gunner's daughter	A flogging

H

Habit	An addiction to narcotics
Hair of the dog	A morning drink of an intoxicant
Haircut	A severe financial loss
Half-inch	To steal
Half-seas over	Drunk
Hammer	To declare a defaulter
Hand	An employee
Hand	The giving of a woman in marriage
Hand in your dinner pail	To die
Handful	A prison sentence of five years
Handout	A payment for which nothing is given in return
Handshake	A supplementary payment on leaving a job
Hang	To kill by breaking the neck through suspension
Hang a few on	To drink intoxicants

Hang a red light on	To drive out of business
Hang in the bell-ropes	To be jilted
Hang on the bough	(of a female) to remain unmarried
Hang out to dry	To expose a person publicly in an attempt to protect others
Hang out with	To enjoy an extramarital sexual relationship with
Hang paper	To issue cheques or other securities fraudulently
Hang up your boots	To retire (from games or sporting activities)
Hang up your hat	To marry a woman much wealthier than yourself
Hang up your hat	To die
Hanky-panky	Extramarital sexual familiarity
Happen to	To cause to die
Happy dust	Cocaine
Happy event	The birth of a child
Happy hour	A period when a bar sells alcohol more cheaply
Happy release	The death of a terminally ill patient
Hard	Denoting an extreme version of anything taboo or shameful
Hard of hearing	Deaf

Hard room	A prison cell
Hard up	Poor
Hardware	Any modern armaments
Harpic	Mentally unbalanced
Harry	The devil
Harvest	To kill for personal gratification
Hatch	The birth of a child
Hatchet (man)	Someone entrusted with a job requiring ruthlessness or destructive criticism
Haute cuisine	Small portions of expensive food
Have a few	To drink intoxicants to excess
Head	A narcotics addict
Headcount management	Dismissing staff
Headhunter	A police internal disciplinary inspector
Headshrinker	A psychiatrist
Health	Illness
Heart (condition)	A malfunction of the heart
Heaven	Associated with the ingestion of illegal narcotics
Heaviness	Obesity
Heavy landing	An aircraft crash on the runway
Heavy of foot	In a late stage of pregnancy
Heel-tap	A small volume of alcohol left in a glass

Heels foremost	Dead
Heightened	Interrogation torture
Heist	Mainly a theft: *a variant of HOIST, referring to taking a truckload of goods or to an armed robbery*
Help	The services of a ghost writer
Help yourself	To steal
Hemp	Pertaining to hanging
Hen	Associated with a bribe
Herb	Marijuana
Hereafter (the)	Death
Hide	To conceal illegally
High	Drunk or under the influence of narcotics
Hijack	To take illegal possession of (a vehicle)
Hike	An unwelcome increase in selling price
Hillside	Men who are outlaws
Hit	To kill
Hit the bottle	To drink intoxicants to excess
Hit the bricks	To escape or desert
Hoist	To rob
Hold paper on	To have a warrant for the arrest of
Hold-up	A robbery
Hold your liquor	To drink a lot of alcohol without appearing drunk

Holiday	A term in prison
Holiday ownership	A compounded annual rent paid in advance
Hollow	Legs; the ability to drink a lot of beer, wine, or spirits and remain sober
Holy of holies	A lavatory
Holy wars	The expansion into the Middle East in the Middle Ages by western adventurers
Home economics	Cooking and house-keeping
Home equity loan	A second mortgage
Homely	Plain-looking (used of women)
Honest	Chaste
Honey trap	An attempt to seduce for subsequent blackmail or exposure
Honour chastity	In a woman
Honours	Rewards
Hook	To steal
Hook	A threat or enticement
Hooker	A prostitute
Hoosegow	A prison
Hospice	An institution for the incurable or dying
Hot	Sexually aroused
Hot place (the)	Hell

Hot seat	An electric chair used for execution/ a guest at a quiz show
House man	A security guard
House of correction	A prison
House-proud	Obsessed with domestic cleanliness and tidiness
Housecleaning	The elimination of undesirable or embarrassing items
Human intelligence	The use of spies: *espionage jargon for the acquisition of intelligence, or information*
Human waste	Sewage
Hush money	A bribe to ensure silence
Hygiene facilities	A lavatory
Hygienic treatment	The temporary preservation of a corpse

I

I hear what you say	I do not agree with you
Ice box	A mortuary
Ice queen	A reserved and chaste young woman
Ideological	Supervision, censorship
Illegal operation	An induced abortion

Little Red Book of Euphemisms 51

Illuminated	Drunk
Imaginative	Journalism sensationalist fabrication
Impaired	Credit carrying a high risk of default
Impaired hearing	Deafness
Impairment	Loss
Improper	Involving promiscuity
Improvement	A reduction in quality or service
Improving knife (the)	Cosmetic surgery
In a pig's ear	No, or that is nonsense
In Abraham's bosom	Dead
In bits	Suffering from a hangover
In Carey Street	Bankrupt
In Dutch	In trouble
In heaven	Dead
In left field	Eccentric or mentally unstable
In season	Able to conceive
In the altogether	Naked
In the arms of Jesus	Dead
In the bag	Taken as a prisoner of war
In the cart	In serious difficulty
In the departure lounge	About to be dismissed from employment

In the family way	Pregnant
In the glue	In personal difficulty
In the red	Owing or losing money
In the ring	Engaged professionally in cheating at auction
In the soil	Dead
In the tank	Drunk
In the trade	Earning a living from prostitution
In years	Old
In your cups	Drunk
Inamorata	A mistress
Incentive	A bribe
Income protection	Arranging your affairs to avoid tax
Incontinent	Promiscuous
Incursion	An unprovoked attack
Indecency	An illegal sexual act
Indescribable	Trousers
Indian hemp	Cannabis
Indigenous	Having remote ancestors from the territory where you live
Indiscretion	A child born out of wedlock
Indisposed	Having a hangover
Inducement	A bribe
Indulge	To drink intoxicants

Little Red Book of Euphemisms 53

Industrial action	A strike
Industrializing country	A poor and relatively undeveloped state
Infidelity	Adultery
Informal	Acting illegally or without required permission
Inner	City slum
Innocence	Virginity
Inquisition	Torture
Inside track	An unfair or illegal advantage
Insider	A person using confidential information for private advantage
Institutionalize	To confine (a person) involuntarily
Intelligence	Spying
Intemperance	Regular drunkenness
Intentions	Whether marriage is proposed
Intermission	A period of television advertisements
Interpret pragmatically	To ignore
Intervention	A military invasion
Intervention	A surgical operation
Introducer's fee	A bribe
Introducing house	A brothel
Intruder	An armed invader

Invalid coach	A hearse
Inventory adjustment	A loss caused from prior overvaluation of goods
Inventory leakage	Stealing
Investment in prices	Price reductions
Invigorating	Cold
Involuntary conversion	An aircraft crash
Irish	Illogical or defective
Irish beauty	A person with two black eyes
Irish confetti	Bricks
Irish hoist	A kick in the pants
Irish horse	An inedible gobbet of meat
Irish hurricane	A calm sea
Irish local	A wheelbarrow
Irish pennant	A loose end
Irish promotion	A reduction in wages
Irish thing (the)	Alcoholism
Irish toothache	Being pregnant
Irish vacation	A term in prison
Irish wedding	The emptying of a cesspit
Irishman's rise	A decrease in pay
Irregular	Acting in a way which breaks taboos

Irreversible coma	Death
Itch	To feel lustful
Itinerant	Irish a gypsy

J

Jack it in	To die
Jag house	A brothel
Jagged	Drunk
Jakes	A lavatory
Jane1	A prostitute
Jane2	A lavatory
Jawbone	Credit: *talk the seller into parting with the goods without paying for them: jawbone*
Jet lag	Disruption of the biological clock through time change on long flights
Jezebel	A prostitute
Jimmy	An act of urination
Job turning	Reducing the responsibility and pay associated with an appointment
John	A lavatory
John Barleycorn	Whisky
Joint	A marijuana cigarette
Jolly	Drunk

Juice	A payment made or demanded illegally
Jump the broomstick	To live together as a couple without marrying
Jump	The last hurdle
Junk	Illegal narcotics

K

Kangaroo	A prison warder
Keel over	To die
Keelhauled	Drunk
Keep up with the Joneses	To live beyond your means or extravagantly
Kick	To die
Kick the habit	To cure yourself an addiction
Kick the tyres	To examine superficially
Kick upstairs	To deprive of power or influence
Kickback	A clandestine illegal payment
Kill a snake	To urinate
Kindness	Bribery
Kingdom	Come death
Kiss the ground	To die
Kitchen-sinking	Making excessive provision
Kite	To issue a negotiable instrument that is not covered by the drawer

Knock down	To kill
Knocking-shop	A brothel
Knuckle sandwich	A punch in the face
Konk off	To die
Korean tartan	An inferior or bogus produce

L

Labor optimization	Matching working hours of employees to demand for their services
Labour	Childbirth
Lack of governance	Incompetence and peculation
Lack of moral fibre	Cowardice
Lack of visibility	Concealment or obfuscation
Ladies' man	A man who delights in the company of women
Lady bear	A policewoman
Lady friend	A female extramarital sexual partner
Lady-in-waiting	A concubine in the Japanese court
Laid to rest	Dead
Lame duck	The holder of an office to which he has not been re-elected
Lame duck	A failing enterprise

Land of forgetfulness (the)	Death
Land of Nod (the)	Sleep
Landscaped	Tidied up
Language	Swear words
Lard the books	Dishonestly to increase a claim for repayment
Last call (the)	Death
Last waltz	The walk to death by execution
Latchkey	Arriving at an empty home
Late	Dead
Late developer	A poor scholar
Laughing academy	An institution for the mentally ill
Launder	To bring funds dishonestly obtained into apparently legal circulation or account
Lavabo	Lavatory
Lavatory	A room set aside for urination and defecation
Lay paper	To pass worthless financial instruments
Leaner	A cheat at cards
Leap the broomstick	To live together as a couple without marrying
Learn on the pillow	To acquire proficiency in a foreign language from a (sexual) mistress who is a native speaker

Learner	A child at school
Leave of absence	Suspension from employment during investigation of a supposed offence
Led astray	Having voluntarily done something for which you later express regard or shame
Left-footer	A person not conforming to the practices or beliefs of the majority
Left-handed	Indicating illegitimacy
Left-handed wife	A woman living with a man to whom she is not married
Leg it	To make an escape
Lend	To lose ownership of
Libel chill	The censorship or suppression of news
Liberate	To conquer
Lick the dust	To die
Lid	An ounce of marijuana
Lift the books	To withdraw from regular service at a church
Lift your little finger	To drink intoxicants
Light-fingered	Thieving
Light-footed	Promiscuous
Light in the head	Of low intelligence
Light on his toe	Homosexual

Limb of the law	A policeman
Limited edition	A publication
Line your pocket	Wrongfully to enrich yourself
Linen	A shirt
Link price	To arrange an illegal cartel
Linked with	Having a sexual relationship with
Liquid	Consisting of, serving, or containing alcohol
Liquidate	To kill, other than by process of law
Little boys' room	A lavatory of exclusive male use
Little gentlemen in back velvet	A mole
Little house	A lavatory
Little Mary	The stomach
Little people	The fairies
Little something	An intoxicant
Little stranger	An unborn child
Little woman	A mistress
Live as man and wife	To cohabit and regularly copulate without being married
Live by trade	To be a prostitute
Live-in girlfriend	A mistress

Little Red Book of Euphemisms 61

Lived-in	Untidy
Load-shedding	A failure of the electricity grid through inability to generate sufficient power
Local	An inn
Lone parent	A parent living alone with dependent offspring
Long home (your)	Death
Long illness (a)	Cancer
Long in the tooth	Old
Long pig	Human flesh
Long-term buy	A poor investment
Longer-living	Geriatric
Loo	A lavatory
Look at the garden	To urinate out of doors
Look in a cup	To foretell the future
Look on the wine when it was red	To be drunk
Loop	To kill by hanging
Loose cannon	A person whose unpredictable conduct may cause difficulties or embarrassment
Lord of the Flies	The devil

Lord sends for you (the)	You are dying
Lose	To dismiss from employment
Lose your lunch	To vomit
Lose your shirt	To be ruined or suffer an excessive financial loss
Loss of separation	Flying dangerously close to another aircraft
Loved one	A dead person
Lover	A male extramarital sexual partner
Low-budget	Cheap
Low flying	Speeding in a motor vehicle
Low profile	With an avoidance of publicity
Lubricate	To bribe or facilitate through bribery
Lucy in the sky with diamonds	Lysergic acid diethylamide
Lump	A corpse
Lunch well	To gormandize at midday
Lunchtime engineering	Bribery
Lush	A drunkard
Lydford law	Arbitrary punishment

M

Maid	A female domestic Servant

Make a call	To urinate: *The CALL OF NATURE, punning on the social visit*
Make a purse for yourself	To seek to engage sexually
Make a purse for yourself	To steal or embezzle
Make away with	To kill
Make off with	To steal
Make old bones	To live long
Make room for tea	To urinate
Make sheep's eyes at	To show sexual interest in (another)
Make the supreme sacrifice	To be killed on war service
Make tracks	To escape or leave in a hurry
Malta dog	Dysentery
Man about town	A philanderer: *literally, a person often seen in society*
Many pounds heavier	Much fatter
March to a different drummer	To be mentally ill: *and out of step*
Margin compression	Adverse trading conditions

Marginalized	Not belonging to a dominant racial or sexual group: *living on the edge of a society*
Marital rights	Copulation by a man with his wife
Mark a card	To register formal dissatisfaction with an employee
Market timing	Dishonestly selecting a favourable price at which to do a deal
Market value adjuster	A penalty imposed by the insurer on those who draw their pensions before the specified date
Martyr to (a)	Suffering from
Mary	Marijuana
Massage	A female domestic servant
Massage	To assault violently: *police jargon for the use of force to obtain information:*
Massage	To overstate or wrongly increase (figures)
Massage parlour	A brothel
Mature	Old: *fully developed mentally*
Maturer	Fatter
Me-too	Exactly copying (of goods and services)
Measure for the drop	To dismiss from employment
Medal showing	A visible undone fly button on trousers

Medical correctness	Not diagnosing patients accurately or treating them wisely
Medicated	Under narcotic influence
Medium machine	An atomic bomb
Meet your Maker	To die
Memorial	Relating to death
Men in sandals	Unworldly philanthropists
Men in suits	Managers or hose in a learned profession other than medicine wealth through skills or physical labour
Men of respect	Members of the Mafia
Men's(room)	A lavatory for male use only
Mental	Suffering from a permanent illness of the mind
Mercy death	The murder of a patient thought to be terminally ill
Merry-begot	Illegitimate
Mess	To act promiscuously
Mexican brown	Marijuana
Mexican raise	A promotion with no increase in pay
Mickey Mouse	Fraudulent
Middle age	The decades prior to becoming a geriatric
Middle-aged spread	Obesity

Midwives' mercy	Infanticide of an unwanted or deformed baby
Militant	A terrorist
Military intelligence	Spying
Militia	An armed body operating outside normal military regulations
Milk	To cheat or defraud
Minor wife	A mistress
Minority	Those of a different colour, religion, or sex from the majority
Misplace	To lose through negligence
Miss the bus	To fail to seize an opportunity
Misspeak	To lie
Mistress	A man's regular extramarital sexual partner
Mitotic disease	Cancer
Mixed heritage	Born to parents of different race
Mobility impaired	Crippled
Modern conveniences	A lavatory and bathroom indoors
Modernization	An expensive change
Molest	To assault sexually
Moll	A prostitute
Molotov cocktail	A simple petrol bomb; Molotov: *Molotov was Stalin's Foreign Minister in the Second World War*

Mom-and-pop	Staid and old fashioned: *aged parents and often of a small retail business*
Monday Morning quarterback	A fantasist who judges by hindsight
Money house	A paying audience
Monkey (the)	Addiction to illegal narcotics
Monkey business	Promiscuity: *literally, any mischief which a monkey might get up to*
Montezuma's revenge	Diarrhoea
Mood freshener	An illicit drug
Moon people	Lunatics
Moonlight	Associated with smuggling
Moonlight	To work at a second job: *work is often done in the evening without paying tax on the earnings*
Moonlight flit	The clandestine departure of an absconding debtor
Moose	a prostitute
More than a (good) friend	A person with whom you have an extramarital sexual relationship
Morning after (the)	A hangover
Moth in your wallet (a)	Stinginess
Mother-in-law	A mixture of old and bitter ale

Mother's blessing	A narcotic administered to a baby: *The blessing was the peace which came from silencing a crying child*
Mother's ruin	Gin
Motion (a)	Defecation
Motion discomfort	Airsickness
Mountain dew	Whisky: *from the process of distillation and the place where it is done*
Mountain sickness	Arrogance
Move your bowels	To defecate
Mr. Big	A criminal boss
Mrs Chant	A lavatory: *rhyming slang for AUNT in female use*
Mrs Duckett	A mild oath
Mrs Grundy	A moralistic bigot and busybody
Muddy	Tipsy
Mudlark	London - a scavenger or thief
Mug	To rob by violence in a public place
Muggy	Drunk: *literally, moist, and usually of the weather Muggy may also mean stupid*
Multicultural	Embracing people of different skin pigmentation
Municipal farm	A prison: *where convicts are put to work*

Muscle	To assault criminally: *from the force used*
Mutt	Deaf
Mutton dressed as lamb	A woman affecting the dress or style of someone much younger
Muzzy	Tipsy

N

Nab	To steal: literally, to catch or arrest
Nall off	Go away
Nancy	A male homosexual
Napoleon's revenge	Diarrhoea: *as suffered by British tourists in France*
Nappy	An infant's towel to contain excreta
Narrow bed	A grave
National assistance	Monies paid by the state to the poor
National savings	Lending to the government
National service	Compulsory conscription into the armed forces
Native	A non-white person
Native elixir (the)	Whiskey
Nature's garb	Nudity
Naughty	Having a reputation for promiscuity

Little Red Book of Euphemisms

Nautch girl	A prostitute
Necessary (house)	Lavatory
Neck	To kiss and caress amorously
Necklace	To murder by igniting a rubber type placed on the shoulders of a victim
Necktie party	A lynching
Negative cash	Debt
Negative containment	A leak of radiation from a nuclear reactor
Negative contribution	A sale at a loss commercial jargon
Negative coping mechanism	Being inept or weak willed
Negative employee situation	The dismissal of staff
Negative growth	A decline
Negative incident	An event which may cause harm or adverse publicity
Negative (income) tax	State payment to the poor
Negative investment return	A loss: *financial jargon of those for whom loss is a taboo word*

Negative patient care outcome	Death
Negative peer pressure	The discouragement of learning
Negative pricing	Selling at a loss
Negatively impacted	Disappointing or loss making
Negatively privileged	Poor
Negotiable	We do not expect to receive the asking price
Negotiate	To yield or appease
Nelson's blood	Rum
Neoplasm	A cancer: *Mainly medical jargon*
Nerve agent	A noxious gas
Nervous breakdown	A severe mental illness
Networking	Using social contacts for political or financial purposes
Natural	Unfavourable: *the coded language of the corporate analyst*
Neutralize	To kill
Never modest	Arrogant
Never-never (the)	A contract for hire-purchase

New	is a code word which should alert us to what is being concealed, as the following examples indicate
New age	The rejection of conventional attitudes
New economic Zones	The barren places to which opponents were exiled
New Labour	Socialist political party
New man	A male in full employment who also shares domestic chores
New Order	A totalitarian state
New Soviet man	A dedicated Communist
Newgate	A prison
News Management	The suppression of information
Nibble	A theft: *usually taking only a part, in the hope that the depredation will pass unnoticed*
Nick	The devil
Nick	To steal
Nick	A police station or prison
Nickel and dime	To short-change or cheat
Night bucket	A receptacle for urine
Night girl	A prostitute
Nightcap	A drink of intoxicant
Nightclub hostess	A prostitute

Nightingale	A police informer
Nil by mouth	Indicating that a patient should be allowed to die
Nineteenth (hole)	The bar at a golf club: *the first eighteen involve striking a ball and walking after it. Occasionally the nineteenth may be where you drink other than in the clubhouse, or what you drink*
Nip	To steal
No better than she should be	Promiscuous: *usually said of a younger woman by an older*
No (spring) chicken	Old: *of women, usually by younger women - No longer in the first flush of youth applies to both sexes*
No Einstein	Unacademic
No active treatment	Indicating that a patient should be allowed to die. Hospital code on the notes of the terminally ill patient, sometime shortened to NAT
No comment	I admit nothing
No-fly zone	A sexually forbidden area
No heeltaps	Everyone must drink what is in their glass: *a heeltap is the layer of leather on the sole of a shoe, hence what is left in the bottom of an unfinished glass*
No longer with us	Dead
No man's land	A lavatory for female use only

No show	The fraudulent use of a name on a pay sheet
Nocturne	Prostitute
Noggin	An intoxicating drink: *originally, an eighth of a pint of any liquid. Now used of any type of beer or spirits, but not of wine*
Non-aligned	Vacillating in allegiance
Non-heart beating donor	A corpse: *the recipient of a transplanted organ, or his relatives*
Non-industrial	Poor and relatively uncivilized
Non-person	A person without civil rights
Non-profit	Avoiding taxation: *not any old loss-making enterprise, but one set up in such a way that the eventual beneficiary avoids tax through a tax-exempt charity*
Non-strategic	Loss making
Nose job (a)	Cosmetic surgery on the nose
Not a great reader	Illiterate
Not all there	Stupid or confused: *it describes a mental state, not that of an amputee*
Not as young as I was	Old
Not long for this world	About to die

Not rocket science	Simple
Not sixteen annas to the rupee	Of low intelligence
Not very well	Very ill
Not with it	Mentally ill or absent-minded
Not available (to comment)	Unwilling to be publicly compromised or shown up
Not invented here	We reject and denigrate all other ideas than our own
Not return calls	To avoid being interviewed
Not seeing anybody	Not involved in any sexual relationship
Nothing intrusive	Indicating that a patient should be allowed to die: *medical direction in the case of a terminally ill patient*
Notice	Dismissal from employment: *shortened form of notice of dismissal*
Nouvelle cuisine	Small portions of food sold at high prices
Nullification	Killing
Number is up (your)	You are about to be killed
Number nine	A laxative
Number one(s)	Urination
Number one	Self-interest
Number two(s)	Defecation: *mainly of small children*

Nurse	To suckle (a baby)
Nursing home	An institution for geriatrics; *literally, a hospital for any sick person*
Nut	A mentally ill person

O

Oblige	To work for someone as a domestic servant
Obtain	To acquire illegally
Occupied	Defeated and annexed
Odorously challenged	Smelly
Of mature years	Old: *indicates not full development but incipient decline*
Off-colour	Vulgar or offensive
Off-colour	Unwell
Off the chandelier	Bogus
Off the payroll	Dismissed from employment
Off the peg	Inferior or ill-cut
Off the reservation	Acting beyond your authority
Off the voting list	Dead
Off the wagon	Habitually drinking alcohol after a period of abstinence
Off the wall	Mentally ill

Off-white wedding	The marriage of a pregnant bride
Oil	A bribe: *a form of GREASE*
Old Adam	A man's lust
Old-fashioned	Derelict real-estate jargon: *applied to houses*
Old maid	An unmarried woman who is unlikely to marry
Old man's friend	Pneumonia: *it is an illness which allows the elderly to die quickly and without much pain*
Old Sparky	Judicial killing by electrocution
Older women	An elderly female
Oldest profession (the)	Prostitution
On health grounds	Through incompetence: *a face-saving formula, implying that the health of the dismissed employee is at risk rather than that of the company*
On heat	Able to conceive
On ice	In prison
On-message	Uncritically obedient to a party line
On the beach	Dismissed from employment
On the black	Working without paying tax: *a development of black market*
On the box	Ill and needy: *the box was the Poor Box kept in church, in which donations for the poor were left*

On the couch	Engaged in casual copulation
On the fly	Without paying tax
On the gallop	Evading capture
On the left	Operating illegally
On the panel	Absent from work through illness
On the parish	Destitute
On the run (of a fugitive)	Trying to avoid capture
On the seat	In the lavatory
On the shelf (of a female)	Unmarried and unlikely to marry
On the skids	Failing
On the square	Living honestly
On the take	Accepting bribes
On the trot	Suffering from diarrhoea: *marking hurried visits to the lavatory*
On the wagon	Refraining from drinking intoxicants
On vacation	In prison
One-armed bandit	A mechanical gambling device: *one pulls the lever and barrels with coloured pictures on them spin to tell one that the one has lost*
One bubble left of level	Mentally abnormal
One foot in the grave	Near death
One for the road	An extra drink of intoxicant before leaving company

One-night stand	A single night of copulation with a chance partner
One o'clock at the waterworks	Your trouser zip is undone
One of us	A person with similar tastes and manners
One over the eight	An excessive intake of intoxicants on a single occasion
One-parent family	A parent living alone with dependent offspring
One too many	An intoxicant taken to excess
Open housing	The banning of restrictions on ownership
Open marriage	A marriage in which neither spouse hides extramarital copulation
Operation (an)	Surgery: *literally, a work, deed, or action*
Operation Defensive Shield	An invasion
Optically challenged	Having defective eyesight
Order of the boot	Summary dismissal from employment
Orphan-hugging	Seeking publicity through a display of compassion: *a practice of western politicians in poor countries when photographers are present*

Other side (the)	Death
Other side of the tracks	The poor section of town
Out of a position	Involuntarily unemployed
Out of circulation	Menstruating
Out of context	Said inadvisedly
Out of the envelope	Acting eccentrically or without authority: *pilots' jargon, the envelope being the parameters within which an aircraft is designed to perform, as to rates of climb, still, turn etc*
Out of your skull	Mentally unwell
Out to lunch	Mentally unstable
Outdoor plumbing	A primitive lavatory
Outplace	To dismiss from employment
Outrage	To copulate with a woman against her will
Outsourcing	Handing management over to or buying services from the private sector
Over-civilized	Decadent
Over familiar	Marking an unwanted sexual approach to female

Over-fond of the bottle	An alcoholic
Over-geared	Insolvent
Over-invoicing	The payment of money additional to the agreed price in a place selected by the recipient
Over-privileged	Rich
Over-refreshed	Drunk
Over the broomstick	Cohabiting and copulating outside marriage
Over the Jordan	Dead
Over the wall	Escaping from prison
Overactive	Naughty
Over the Dionysian rites	To become drunk: *Dionysus discovered the art of wine-making*
Overdose	An attempt at suicide by self-poisoning with drugs
Overdue	Pregnant
Overflight	A spying mission: *literally, crossing a country in the course of a commercial flight by recognized and agreed path*
Overfriendly	Involving sexual impropriety
Overhaul	A dismissal of employees
Owned	Second-hand

Little Red Book of Euphemisms

P

Pacify	To conduct military operation to foreign territory
Pack it in	To die
Package store	Place to which sells intoxicants
Pad	Dishonestly to inflate
Paddy wagon	A police vehicle
Paint the tape	To record deals at fictitious prices
Paint the town red	To carouse
Painted woman	A prostitute
Palm	An indication of bribery
Pancake	The cow dung cakes
Panhandle	To beg in a public place
Pansy	A male homosexual
Panther sweet	Whisky
Paper hanger	A policeman punishing a motorist for speeding
Paper hanger	A person who passes false negotiable instruments ; *usually of cheques which have been stolen or are not covered by deposits*
Paper the house	To fill seats in a theater by giving tickets away
Parallel	Importing illegally or breach of contract

Parallel parking	Having a mistress
Paramour	A person with whom you have a regular extramarital sexual relationship
Parboiled	Drunk: *literally, thoroughly boiled, whence overheated*
Park women	Prostitute
Parlor house	A brothel
Parsley bed	The place where new girl babies are found
Part	To die
Part with Patrick	To abort a foetus prematurely
Partake	To drink alcohol: *in this case sharing a drink*
Partially sighted	Nearly blind
Party girl	A prostitute
Party member	A communist
Patriotic reticence	The suppression of bad new
Patron	A man who keeps a mistress
Pavement girl	A prostitute
Pavement people	Beggars
Paw	To fondle sexually
Pay to visit	To urinate- *to the loo*
Pay lip service	Insincerely to say you agree

Pay nature's (last) debt	To die of natural causes
Pay with the roll of a drum	To avoid payment
Payoff	A bribe or illegal reward
Payroll adjustment	Dismissal of staff
Peace at last	Death
Pear shaped	Unsuccessful
Pee	To urinate
Peeper	A private detective
Peeping tom	A sexual voyeur: *Leofric, the Anglo-Saxon Lord of Coventry agreed to postpone an increase in taxes if his wife, Godiva, rode naked through the streets. The townspeople were forbidden to watch. And how anybody would have known if Tom hadn't peeped is a matter for conjecture*
Peg	To be a drunkard
Peg out	To die
Penitentiary	A prison
People cuts	The dismissal of employees: *industrial jargon. The term is not used by surgeons*
People's army	An army pledged to the support of a regime when the former non-political or professional army has been disbanded

People's court	A tribunal supporting the regime without trained judges or juries, and without justice or mercy
People's democracy	An autocracy
People's government	A totalitarian tyranny
People's Justice	Summary killed without trial
People's lottery	A national lottery operated by a licensee
People's militia	An armed force supporting those who have seized power
People's palace	A mansion for the exclusive use of an autocrat
People's party	A political grounding
People's tribunal	A political court
Period	The time of menstruation
Permissive	Less constrained by custom in personal conduct
Persona non grata	Someone caught spying
Personal correction	Flogging
Personal representatives	Those who administer the estate of a person who dies intestate or without a living executor
Personality	A nonentity

Personnel ceiling reduction	The dismissal of employees
Pet	To caress physically during courtship
Petite	Very small
Petite amie	A mistress
Petrified	Drunk: *showing no sign of movement, as if turned into stone*
Petticoat	Dominated by a female
Petting stone	A stone at the church gate at which a bride supposedly pronouncedly renounced her ill humours
Phantom	A person paid while not working or nonexistent employee whose wage is drawn by another
Phoenix	Seeking to avoid the payment of liabilities
Physic	A laxative
Pick	To steal
Pick a daisy	To urinate
Pick-me-up	A drink of an intoxicant: *literally, a medicine taken as a tonic, whence jokingly used of spirits*
Pick up	To acquire a sexual partner casually
Pickled	Drunk
Pie-eyed	Drunk: *unable to focus rather than with eyes like pies*

Piece of the action	A share in the proceeds or enjoyment of vice, illegality, or any taboo activity
Piece off	To bribe
Pigeon	The dupe of a criminal
Piggyback	To use another's reputation for your financial or social ends
Pill	A contraceptive taken orally by females
Pillow partner	A person with whom you copulate
Pin-up	An erotic picture
Pinch	To steal: *literally, to nip between the fingers*
Ping-ponging	Passing a rich client from one specialist to another: a medical version of the long rallies in table tennis
Pink	Associated with male homosexuality
Pink slip	A notice of dismissal
Pissed	Drunk
Pit-stop	An occasion for leaving company for a short taboo activity
Place-man	A spy
Place of ill fame	A brothel
Planned parenthood	The abortion of a foetus

Plasma	An intoxicant; *literally, the covered with a substance in the blood in which other elements are suspended*
Plastered	Drunk
Plastic chicken circuit (the)	Dinners organized by institutions
Play about	To fool around with the other sex
Play round	To be promiscuous, usually of a male
Play away (from home)	To commit adultery
Play games	To be promiscuous
Play hookie	To commit adultery
Play house	A brothel
Play the goat	To be promiscuous
Play a card	To deploy an argument based on prejudice or emotion
Play back	To provide information through an enemy spy
Play boy	The devil
Pledge	An undertaking never to drink intoxicants
Plough	To fail a candidate in and examination
Plug	To kill by shooting
Plumbing	A lavatory
Pocket	To steal
Poetic truth	Lies
Point shaving	Fraudulently reducing the margin of victory

Political change	A humiliating defeat
Politically correct	Conforming in behavior or language to domestic opinions
Polygraph	A lie detector
Poodle	A sycophant
Pooped	Drunk: *originally, flooded by the sea coming over the stern, but not only of sailors*
Pop off	To die
Post-war credit	A tax
Postal	Mentally unstable
Posterior (s)	The buttocks
Pot	Marijuana
Pot hunter	An egoist seeking public recognition
Potation	An alcoholic drink
Potboiler	A repetitive or facile work by an established artist or author
Potentially ineffective care	Not allowing the mortally ill to die
Potomac fever	Desire to be elected to high Federal office
Pouch	To steal
Pound salt	Go away and leave me alone
Pourboire	A bribe
Powder	A narcotic taken illegally

Powder room	A lavatory for the exclusive use of females
Prairie-dogging	Unnecessarily standing up to look over the partition of a work station
Prairie oyster	A pungent alcoholic drink with a raw egg in it
Pre-arrangement	The payment for a funeral before death
Precautions	Contraception
Precocious	Spoilt and ill-mannered
Premature	Conceived before marriage
Premium	Costing more
Prepared biography	A draft obituary of a living person
Present	A bribe: *the gift is a payment for a service which should be provided free*
Preventative	Contraceptive sheathe
Prey to (a)	Suffering from
Prima donna	A prostitute
Prime	Saleable
Primed	Drunk
Prince of darkness	The devil
Princess	An expensive prostitute
Private enterprise	Illegal trading by an employee
Pro-choice	In favour of abortion on demand

Problem	An unwanted and often irreversible condition
Proclivities	Unconventional sexual preferences
Procure	To a arrange (prostitution) on behalf of another
Product	A service
Product placement	Securing media exposure of an article on sale
Product shrinkage	The supply of a lesser quantity at the previous price
Production difficulties	Strikes
Profession (the)	Female prostitution
Professional car	A hearse
Progressive	Opposed to conventional manners or methods
Proletarian	Communist
Promoted to Glory	Dead
Pronounce	To confirm the death of
Proper	Chaste
Prophylactic	A contraceptive sheath
Proposition selling	The use of misleading: *hypotheses to confuse a buyer*
Public assistance	Money paid regularly by the state to the needy

Public convenience	A lavatory
Public house	An establishment where intoxicant may be sold and drunk
Public ownership	Control and management by politicians and bureaucrats
Public-private partnership	Accepting private finance and management for a public service
Public sector borrowing requirement	Government overspending
Pull	To cause a horse to lose a race
Pull out of a hat	To produce irresponsibly: *as the conjurer produces the rabbit*
Pull rank	To use seniority to secure an unfair advantage
Pull the pin	To retire from employment
Pull the plug on	To kill by withdrawing mechanical life support
pull the rug	To render bankrupt
Punk	Low-quality marijuana
Puppy fat	In a child
Push	A sustained attack in war
Push the button on	To kill or cause to be killed
Put a move on	To make a sexual approach
Put (a person's) lights out	To kill

Put against a wall	To kill
Put away	To kill
Put daylight through	To kill by shooting
Put down	To kill
Put in the mobility pool	Summarily dismissed from employment
Put in your ticket	To die
Put on file	Rejected for employment
Put on the spot	To kill
Put out of your troubles	To kill
Put out to grass	To cause to retire from work prematurely
Put the boot in	To disrupt or upset through offensive behaviour or the threat of violence
Put the clock back	Fraudulently to alter the reading of a milometer
Put the clog in	Deliberately to injure an opposing player
Put the juice to	To kill by electrocution
Put to rest	Dead
Put to sleep	To kill
Put to the question	To torture

Put to the sword	To kill
Put under the sod	Dead

Q

Qualify accounts	To throw doubt on published figures
Quality time	A period sacrificed to being with your young child or children
Quantitatively challenged	Obese
Queen	A prostitute
Queen	A male homosexual
Queen's evidence	Betraying a fellow malefactor
Queer	Drunk
Queer	Of unsound mind
Queer	Homosexual
Quench your thirst	To drink alcohol to excess
Questionable	Immoral or illegal
Quick (with child)	Pregnant
Quick one	A drink of intoxicant
Quiescent	In a flaccid state
Quiet	To die

Quod	Prison

R

Rabbit	An incompetent performer in sport
Racial	Displaying prejudice against or hostility towards an ethnic group
Racism	Intolerance towards or ill-treatment of those of a different race or nationality
Racist	An intolerant bigot in matters of race and nationality
Racked	Drunk or under the influence of illegal narcotics
Radical	Accepting or advocating extreme political policies
Railroad bible	A pack of playing cards
Rainbow fascist	An intolerant person obsessed with ecological matters
Raincoat	A male contraceptive sheath
Rainmaker	A person valued in an organization primarily for his contacts
Ramp	To rob, cheat, or overcharge
Rap club	A brothel
Rational	Agreeing with a prejudice
Rationalize	Arbitrarily to reduce
Raunchy	Lustful or pornographic
Ravish	To copulate with a woman against her will

Raw	Naked
Razor	To maim or kill by cutting
Reading Geneva print	Drunk
Realign	To devalue
Reaper(the)	Death
Rears	Lavatories
Rebalance	To increase: *of prices, when the balance is always heavier rather than lighter*
Rebase	To reduce
Receding (hairline)	Baldness
Receiver	A dealer in stolen property
Receiver general	A prostitute
Recent unpleasantness	A war
Rectification of frontiers	The annexation of territory by force
Red	An allusion to menstruation
Red card	To dismiss or deny entry to
Red cross	Morphine
Red eye	Poor-quality potable alcohol
Red ink	An indication of loss
Red lamp	A brothel
Redeployed	Dismissed from employment

Redistribution of wealth	Punitive taxation
Redlining	Refusing credit solely because of the place of residence of the applicant
Redneck	A poorly educated and bigoted white man
Reduce the headcount	To dismiss employees
Redundant	Dismissed from employment
Reefer	A marijuana cigarette
Reengineer	Summarily to dismiss employees
Refer to drawer	This cheque is unpaid through lack of funds
Refresh your memory	To correct previous perjury
Refresher	A drink of an intoxicant
Regular	Small
Relief	Public aid given to the indigent
Originally	A feudal payment to an overlord on coming into an estate
Relinquish	To leave after being dismissed
Relocate	To dismiss from employment
Removal	A murder
Removal	Dismissal from employment
Remunerated balances	Credit accounts on which interest is paid
Repositioning	The dismissal of staff
Reshuffle	To dismiss from employment

Resign	To be dismissed from employment
Resign your spirit	To die
Resistance	Any dissent or divergence
Rest room	A lavatory
Resting	Unemployed
Restorative art	Embalming: *funeral jargon*
Retainer	A series of payments made to an extortionist: *literally, a sum paid to retain the service of a lawyer*
Retard	A simpleton
Retire	To dismiss from employment
Retread	A single woman who has previously lived with a man in a sexual relationship
Retrenched	Dismissed from employments
Return fire	To attack without warning
Revenue enhancement	Raising taxes
Reverse engineering	Unauthorized copying
Reviver	A drink of an intoxicant
Revolving door	Involving excessive change of management
Rib joint	A brothel
Rich friend	A man with a much younger mistress
Richness of stock	An excess inventory

Ride backwards	To be taken to your execution
Ride the horse	To menstruate
Right-sizing	The dismissal of employee
Ripples on (have)	To be mildly drunk
Roach	A cockroach
Road apples	Horse turds in the street
Road is up for repair (the)	I am menstruating
Rob the cradle	To from a sexual attachment with a much younger person
Rollicked	Drunk
Roman candle	A failure of a parachute
Roman spring (a)	Lust in the elderly: *it attempts to do for geriatrics what an Indian summer does for the climate*
Romp	To copulate
Roof rabbit	A cat
Rope (the)	Death by hanging
Roses	Menstruation
Rough trade	An uncouth male in a sexual role
Round the bend	Mentally unbalanced
Roving eye	A tendency towards promiscuity
Rubber	A contraceptive sheath
Rubber cheque	A cheque which is dishonoured

Rubber heel	A detective: *from their habit of walking around quietly*
Rumble	To steal
Run away	Permanently to leave the matrimonial home
Runny nose	An addiction to cocaine
Runny tummy (a)	Diarrhoea
Rush the growler	To send for beer to drink at home: *a growler is a large pitcher. If you dallied on the return journey, the beer might become warm.*
Rusticate	To banish

S

Sack (the)	Dismissal from employment
Sacrifice Your Honour	(of a female) to copulate outside marriage
Saddle Soap	Flattery
Safe House	A refuge
Safe Sex	Sexual activity with another in which a prospective sheath is used
Safety Camera	A roadside radar camera recording vehicle speed
Salami	Achieving an unpopular or deceitful result by small increments
Salt	To cheat by improper addition
Sanitary Man	A cleaner of lavatories

Sanitary Towel	An absorbent padding worn during menstruation
Sanitized	Cleaned or rendered harmless
Sappho	A homosexual female
Sarah	A wealthy divorced woman
Sartorially challenged	Badly dressed
Satisfaction	The acceptance of a challenge to a dual whatever outcome
Sauna	A brothel
Say a Few Words	To make a speech
Say Goodbye to	To dismiss from employment
Scandal Sheet	A form on which expenses are claimed
Scarlet Women	A prostitute
Scissor-And-Paste Job	A book or article not based on original research
Scoop	An alcoholic drink
Scope For Modernization	Ramshackle
Scorch Eliminator	A fire extinguisher
Scorched	Drunk or under the influence of illegal narcotics
Scotch Mist	Drunk
Scrag	To kill

Screw (of a male)	To copulate with
Screw Loose (a)	Mental instability
Screwed	Drunk
Scrubber	A prostitute
Scuttered	Drunk
Seasonal ownership	An entitlement to occupy for a limited period
Seduce	To persuade a woman to copulate with you extra martially
See a man about a dog	To go to any place that is the subject of taboo or embarrassment
See the rose bed (of a male)	To urinate out of doors
Seen better days	Poor
Seepage	The amount stolen from a retail store: *literally, the liquid which has slowly escaped from a container*
Segregation	The availability of inferior facilities for a minority ethnic group
Select	Capable of being offered for sale
Selected out	Dismissed from employment
Self-defence	An unannounced military attack
Self-deliverance	Suicide

Semi-detached (of a house)	Sharing a party wall
Send down	To dismiss
Send in your papers	(Of an officer) to retire prematurely
Send to heaven	To kill
Send to the showers	To dismiss from a game
Senior citizen	An old person
Senior Moment (a)	Temporary forgetfulness
Sensible	Unfashionable but practical
Sensitive payment	A tribe
Sent home in a body bag	Killed
Separate	To cease living together as man and wife
Separate but equal	Subject to inferior and humiliating treatment
Service	A charge addition to the cost of the goods supplied
Service Lawyer	A clerk in a law office
Services no Longer Required	Dismissed from employment
Settle	To kill

Settle	To conquer and appropriate
Seven Year Itch	A wish for extramarital sexual variety after a period of a steady marriage
Severance	Dismissal from employment
Sewage	A noxious domestic discharge
Sewn up	Pregnant
Sexual ambiguity	Having bisexual tastes
Sexual assault	An unsuccessful attempt at rape
Sexual preference	Homosexuality
Shake up (with)	To cohabit in an extramarital sexual relationship
Shake hands with the Bishop (of a male)	To urinate
Shake the Pagoda Tree	To make a rapid fortune in India
Shanghai	Forcibly to abduct a person
Share (someone's) affections	To have an open adulterous relationship
Sheath	A contraceptive worn by a male
Sheep buck	A ram
Sheep's eyes (make)	To indicate sexual attraction in a look

Sheet in the wind (a)	Mildly drunk
Shellacked	Very drunk literally: *covered with shellac, a varnish which is stoved to give a glazed appearance*
Shelved	Dismissed from employment
Sheriff's hotel	A prison
Shift expenses	Improperly seek to avoid the payment of higher taxes or interest charges
Shoo-in	A favored successor
Shoot (the)	Peremptory dismissal from employment
Shoot	To inject an illegal narcotic
Shoot a line	To boast
Shoot the cat	To become drunk: *originally, to vomit, from a similar tendency in cats*
Shoot with a silver gun	To be unable to provide meat by hunting
Shop	To give information leading to arrest
Shop door is open (the)	Your trousers are unfastened
Shoplift	To pilfer from a shop
Short	A handgun
Shortened the front (line)	To retreat under pressure
Shorten the front (line)	To loose weight punning on the military euphemism and usually of men
Shortism	The pursuit of quick profit

Shot	A measure of spirits
Shot in the tail	Pregnant
Shot while trying to escape	Murdered in custody
Shotgun marriage	The marriage of a pregnant bride to the putative father
Shout (the)	Peremptory dismissal from employment: *Dismissed employees may say they have had the shout even if dismissed sotto voce or in writing*
Shout	An obligation to pay for a round of drinks in a bar
Show the door	To dismiss peremptorily from employment
Shrinkage	The amount stolen from retail stores
Shroud waving	A tactic for safeguarding or augmenting expenditure on medical projects or the salaries of those employed in the industry
Sick-out	A strike by public service employees
Sight-deprived	Blind
Sing (of criminal)	To give information to the police
Sing a different tune	To change your story, attitude, or opinion
Single parent	A parent living with dependent offspring without an adult partner
Sink	A lavatory

Siphon off	To steal
Sitting by the window	Underemployed
Six feet of earth	Death
Six o'clock swill	An excessive drinking or beer
Sizzle	To be killed by electrocution
Skin of all dead horses	To marry your mistress
Skinful	An excessive quantity of intoxicating drink
Skinny-dip	To bathe in the nude
Skivvy	A prostitute
Sky-piece	A wig
Slammer	A prison
Slapper	A prostitute
Slash and burn	Asset stripping and ruthless cost-cutting: *financial jargon copied from primitive agriculture*
Slate-off	A person with low intelligence or lacking common sense
Sledge	Unsporting to harass (an opponent)
Sleep over	To stay overnight for extramarital sexual activity
Slewed	Drunk

Slice	To cheat (a customer): *retailer's jargon for overcharging by removing a silver of cheese etc. from what has been weighted and priced*
Slight chill	A pretext for not keeping an engagement
Slippage	Mental illness or decline
Sloshed	Drunk
Slow	Stupid
Slowdown	A deliberate failure to do work for which you are being paid
Sluice	A lavatory
Slush	Bribery
Smack	Illegal heroin
Small folk (the)	The fairies
Small print	Onerous condition in a contract which are not given prominence
Smallest room (the)	The lavatory
Smalls	Underpants and brassieres
Smashed	Drunk or under the influence of illegal narcotics
Smear	To bribe
Smear out	To kill
Smell	To be tainted with
Smithfield bargain	A marriage to secure wealth

Smoke	To murder
Smoke and mirror	Deception
Smoker	The devil
Smoking gun (a)	Conclusive evidence of guilt
Smooth	To distort (published accounts)
Smut house	A place where pornographic programmes are screened
Snaffle	To steal
Snag	To pilfer
Snack oil	Something worthless or deceitful
Snake pit	A mental hospital
Snatch	To steal
Sneezer	A prison
Sniff	To inhale narcotics or stimulants illegally
Snifter	A drink of spirits
Snout	Tobacco
Snug	Inconveniently
So-and-so	A mild insult
So-so	In a physical condition which differs from the normal
Soak	A drunkard
Social agenda	An attempt to impose conformity
Social cohesion	The absence of hostility between ethnic groups

Social evil (the)	Prostitution
Social fairness	Giving favourable treatment to the poor
Social housing	Accommodation built with the aid of subsidy for poor people
Social inclusion	Giving special advantages to selected group of people
Social justice	An imprecise dogma based on a wish to improve the situation of the poor rather than on the rule of law
Social ownership	Control by politicians and bureaucrats
Social rented home	A house let at less than the market price
Social security	The payment of money by the state to the poor
Social services	An institution of the state for dealing with the young
Socialist justice	Arbitrary punishment
Socially excluded	Poor
Soft commission	A bribe
Soft-shoe	A clandestine or indirect approach
Soft skill	Application and discipline
Soft soap	Flattery
Softness in the economy	A recession
Soil	Excrement

Soiled dove	A prostitute
Solicit	To offer sexual services for money
Solid waste	Human excrement
Solidarity	Participating in a strike on behalf of others
Something for the weekend	A contraceptive sheath
Something on you	Damaging piece of knowledge about you
Son of the bitch	An illegitimate child
Sop	A drunkard
Sot	A drunkard
Sought after	Expensive
Sound bite	A spoken phrase or sentence short and pithy enough to be broadcast in its entirety
Source	An associate briefed to give confidential information
Sow your wild oats	To behave wildly or irresponsibly
Sozzle	To drink to excess
Spanish tummy	Diarrhoea
Speak with forked tongue	To dissimulate serpents want to have a word with animal rights enthusiasts about this usage, without which writers of screenplays for westerns would have had to dream up another cliché

Little Red Book of Euphemisms

Special area	A region of economic decline and relative poverty
Special Branch	Police dealing with subversion and terrorism
Special camp	A place for the arbitrary imprisonment of potential enemies
Special friend	A sexual partner to whom you are not married
Special investigations unit	Malefactors for political purposes
Special needs	Requiring extra facilities and attention
Special operations	Something illegal or secret
Special police	Police seconded from normal duties to control subversion and political disorder
Special weapon	Missiles with nuclear explosive warheads
Speed money	Bribes
Spend a penny	To urinate
Spend more time with your family	To be dismissed from employment
Spin a line	To boast
Spirits	Spirituous intoxicant
Splash	To crash into the sea

Splash your boots	To urinate
Sponge	A habitual drunkard
Sponsor	An advertiser
Sports medicine	Illegal drugs
Spur of the moment passion	Unpremeditated extramarital copulation
Spurious	Illegitimate
Squash	To kill
Squeal (of a criminal)	To give information to the police
Squeeze	To extort from illegally
Squeeze	An attempted deflationary measure
Squiffy	Drunk
Squirrel	The patient of a psychiatrist The animal has a penchant for a NUT A squirrel tank is an institute of the insane
Stabilization	Price control by government
Stalk	To harass obsessively
Stand before your maker	To die
Stand down	To be dismissed or prematurely retired from employment

Stand up	Without notice or apology to fail to keep a date with (someone)
Stand-up	A person paid to make an instant comment on television
Standard	Small or poor quality
Standstill	An attempt by government to restrict pay increases
Star in the east(a)	An undone-fly-button
Stark	Naked
Start bleeding	To menstruate for the first time
Starter (home)	A small house
Stash	A supply of illegal narcotics
State of armed conflict	A war
State of nature (a)	Nudity
Statutory offense	The rape of a female
Step down	To be dismissed from employment
Step-ins	Women's underpants
Step on	To kill
Stepney	A pimp's favourite prostitute
Sterilize	To destroy
Stewed	Drunk
Stews (the)	A brothel

Stick	A marijuana cigarette Also known as a stick of tea, dream stick, or punning joy-stick To stick a drink is to add spirits to it
Sticky-fingered	Thieving or corrupt
Sticky floor	A low: *paid job in which certain categories of employee may remain indefinitely*
Stiff one	A drink of spirits
Stimulant (a)	Spirits or an illegal narcotic
Sting	To deprive by trickery
Stinking	Very drunk
Stitch up	To fabricate evidence against
Stitched	Drunk
Stoat	A libertine
Stoned	Drunk or under the influence of illegal narcotics
Stool pigeon	A police informer
Story	A lie
Straighten out	To bribe: *Straighten the line to retreat under pressure*
Strain credulity	To be considered untruthful
Stranger to the truth	A habitual liar

Strategic	Is an adjective which should always put us on the alert. It means according to a plan but more often seeks to indicate failure or an action taken under compulsion
Strategic differences	Arguments between managers or politicians; more often over personalities than plans
Strategic movement to the rear	A defeat in battle
Strategic premium	An overpayment
Strategic review	A commercial inquest An exercise when managers try to discover why they are in difficulty and whom they can blame
Strategic withdrawal	A retreat
Streak	To run naked in a public place
Streamline	To dismiss
Stretch	A period of imprisonment
Stretch the hemp	To kill by hanging
Stretcher	A lie or exaggeration: *Stretching the truth and those who do it are punning stretcher cases*
String up	To kill by hanging

Stripper	A thief - especially of radios etc. from cars
	In standard English, a stripper removes clothes for sexual titillation
Strong waters	Spirituous intoxicants
Stump liquor	Illegal spirits
Stunt	A limited drunk
Stunted hare	A rabbit
Stupid	Drunk
Subnormal	Suffering from mental illness or disability
Sub-prime	Not creditworthy
Subsidy publishing	The publication of a book at the author's expense
Substance	An illegal narcotic
Succumb	To die
Suffer fools gladly	To tolerate incompetence
Sugar	A bribe
Sugar	A mild oath: *Common genteel use, for the taboo shit*
Sugar daddy	A man with mistress much younger than himself
Sun has been hot today	There are signs of drunkenness
Sun is over the yardarm	Let us drink some alcohol

Sunday traveller	An illegal drinker of intoxicants at an inn
Sundowner	A drink of intoxicants
Sunset years	Old age
Supplier discount	A preferential price
Supporters club	Investors who act in concert
Supreme measure of punishment	Death by execution
Sure thing	A promiscuous woman
Surplus	A profit
Surveillance	Spying
Suspect cigarette	An illegal narcotic
Swallow the anchor	To retire from a career at sea
Swallow the Bible	To perjure yourself
Sweat it out of	To obtain information from by coercion
Sweet equity	Shares issued to favoured parties at below their value
Sweet man	A woman's regular extra marital sexual partner
Sweetbreads	Animal glands used for good: *Literally, the thymus or pancreas, but also the testicles*

Sweeten	To bribe
Sweeten	To attempt to improve by deception
Sweetheart	Indicative of an arrangement which improperly benefits two parties at the expense of a third
Swell	To be pregnant
Swill	To be a habitual drunkard
Swing the lamp	To boast
Swipe	To steal
Switch-selling	Dishonest advertising of cheap goods designed to induce a customer to buy something dearer
Syndrome	Any taboo medical condition
Synergy benefit	The dismissal of employees

T

Tactical	Done involuntarily under pressure
Tagged	Hit by a bullet
Tail	To follow surreptitiously
Tail-pulling	The publication of a book at the author's expense
Take a bath	To suffer a heavy financial loss - your boast is capsized
Take a break	To allow the intrusion of advertisements Television jargon, especially when the same programme will be resumed

Take a drink	To be an alcoholic
Take a hike	To leave in a hurry
Take a leap	To kill yourself by jumping off a high place
Take a walk	To leave involuntarily or under taboo circumstance
Take a wheel off the cart	To force another into bankruptcy
Take electricity	To be judicially killed
Take for a ride	To murder
Take refuge in a better world by your own hand	To kill yourself
Take the can back	To be held responsible
Take the Fifth	To decline to testify in court. The Fifth amendment to the constitution of United States provides that witness cannot be forced to give testimony which may incriminate themselves
Take the pants off	To reduce to penury
Take the wind	To be summarily dismissed from employment or courtship
Take to the cleaners	To rob or cheat
Take to the hills	To escape or absent yourself for a taboo reason

Tampax time	The period of menstruation of obvious derivation
Tanked (up)	Under the influence of alcohol or narcotics
Tarbrush (the)	Partial descent from a non-white ancestor
Tart	A prostitute or promiscuous person
Taskforce	A committee hastily summoned to deflect attention from previous incompetence
Tea	Marijuana
Tea Leaf	A thief
Tea money	A bribe or tip
Technical adjustment	A sudden fall in stock market prices
Technicolor yawn (a)	Vomiting due to drunkenness
Teflon	Able to avoid responsibility
Ten commandments (the)	Scratches by a woman's fingernails
Ten one hundred	Stopping at the roadside to urinate
Tender a fool	To give birth to an illegitimate child
Tenderloin	Associated with promiscuity and other illegality
Tenure	A job for life
Testing	Unfavourable

Thai stick	A cigarette composed of an illegal narcotic
Thick of hearing	Deaf
Third degree	Police violence to extract information
Third party payment	A bribe
Third world	Poor
Three-letter man	A swindler or cheat
Three pennies (the)	British diarrhoea
Throw the book at	To charge with every feasible offence
Throw the switches	To become mentally unbalanced
Throw up	To vomit
Thunder box	A port lavatory
Tick	A person clandestinely following another
Ticker	The heart
Tickle	To caress sexually
Tiddly	Slightly drunk
Tie a can on	To dismiss from employment
Tiger-sweat	An impure intoxicant
Tight	Drunk

Tight	Stingy
Tin year (a)	Arrogant disregard
Tin handshake	A derisory payment on dismissal from employment. He who leaves would prefer it to be GOLDEN
Tincture	A partial descent from other than white ancestry: *Literally, pigment, and used offensively of those whose dark skin pigmentation indicates a non-white ancestor*
Tinker	A gypsy or itinerant at one time he made a living travelling from door to door mending pans mainly derogatory use
Tin pot	Pretentiously assuming the trappings and manner of authority
Tint	To dye (hair)
Tipple	An intoxicating drink
To one side of the truth	Untrue
To the knuckle	Devoid of resources all the meat has gone
Toilet	A lavatory
Tollbooth	A prison
Tomboy	A prostitute
Tongue	An enemy prisoner captured for interrogation
Too busy to take/return call	Unwilling to speak to a journalist

Top shelf	Pornographic
Top up	To conceal inferior goods below those of higher quality
Topless	Exposing your breasts in public
Torch	To set light to as an arsonist
Tot	A drink of spirits: *Literally, anything small, whence a small drinking vessel or measure, which used to be from quarter to half a pint. Formerly, to tot was to drink intoxicants*
Touch signature	A fingerprint
Touched (in the head)	Mentally ill
Toy boy	A man consorting sexually with a much older woman
Trains potter	A boring person
Transfer pricing	The fraudulent adjustment of price between connected companies in different jurisdictions so as to reduce outgoings
Travel expenses	Bribes or money claimed dishonestly
Treasonable activity	Losing a battle or retreating
Treat	To bribe
Treatment	The use of violence to extract information

Tree-hugger	A person thought to be unduly obsessed with preservation of the environment
Triangular	Where two people with to enjoy an exclusive sexual relationship with a third
Tribute	A regular payment to an extortionist
Trip	A condition induced by the ingestion of illegal hallucinogens
Trophy	Advertising your wealth and status something which can be flaunted to indicate great wealth or fame
Trots (the)	Diarrhoea
Truth shader	A liar
Tub of grease	A place or situation where corruption is endemic
Tuft-hunter	A sycophant
Turf accountant	A person who accepts bets for a living
Turkey shoot	A business easily concluded
Turkish ally	An unreliable supporter
Turkish medal	An inadvertently exposed
Turn up your toes	To die
Twelve annas to the rupee	Of mixed Indian and white ancestry
Twenty four hour service	We have a telephone recording

| Twilight home | An institution for the geriatric. Not a summer house facing the west but from the cliché twilight of your life |

U

U-turn	A fundamental change of policy
Uganda	Promiscuous sexual relationship
Unaddressed	Sent as unsolicited advertising matter
Unassigned	Dismissed from employment
Uncle1	A pawnbroker
Uncle tom	A black person who defers unduly to whites
Under-invoicing	Fraudulent device to avoid import duties
Under the counter	Illegal
Under the daisies	Dead
Under the table	Very drunk
Under the table	Illicit
Under the weather	Unwell
Underachiever	An idle or stupid child
Under-developed	Poor

Undertaker	A professional who arranges of funerals
Under-privileged	Poor
Undisciplined	Neglected and overgrown
Undocumented	Arriving without proper authority
Uneven	Bad
Unfair	Economically embarrassing
Unfaithful	Having had a sexual relationship with other than your regular sexual partner
Unfortified	Not having drunk alcohol
Unglued	Mentally ill. Your mind had become unstuck
Unheard presence	Someone dismissed from employment
Unhinged	A police officer
University	A political prison
Unlawful	Illegitimate
Unofficial action	A strike in breach of an agreement
Unofficial relations	Corrupt practices
Unplugged	Mentally ill
Unprotected sex	Copulation without a condom
Unscrewed Mad	What happens after you have a SCREW LOOSE

Unsighted	Blind
	Literally, prevented from seeing by an intervening obstruction
Unsalted	Of unsound mind
Unsound	Not to be trusted
Unwired	Mentally unbalanced like an electrical device which is not connected to a power supply
Up the loop mad	The imagery was from railway shunting practices, where a wagon might be misdirected on to the wrong loop, or siding
Upstairs	Death
Use your tin	To identify yourself as a policeman
Used	Second-hand
Useful expenditure	A bribe
Useful girl	A domestic servant. The phrase avoids any implication of subservience

V

Vaccum	To destroy incriminating evidence
Valentine	A warning or notice of dismissal
Vanity publishing	The publishing of a book or article at the author's expense where the venture is not commercially attractive to a professional publisher

Vatican roulette	The use of the safe period method of contraception
Velvet	Obtained gratuitously
Ventilate	To kill
Verbal	An oral admission of guilt
Verbally deficient	Unable to read
Vertically challenged	Of short stature
Vicar of bray	A cowardly or opportunistic trimmer
Vigorous	Promiscuous
Visually challenge	Ugly
Visually impaired	Blind or with very poor eyesight
Vital statistics	The measurement of a woman's chest, waist, and buttocks
Voice risk analysis	Lie detection

W

Wages of sin (the)	Death
Walk (the streets)	To be a prostitute
Walk out	To go on strike
Walk out with	To court

Walk the plank	To be killed by drowning
Wall-eyed	Drunk
Wallflower	A young woman who is failing to attract a male companion
Wander	To philander within marriage
Wandering eye	A tendency to promiscuity
Wang-house	A brothel
Want	To lust after
Warm (with wine)	Tipsy
Warm a bed	To copulate with someone promiscuously
Warm up old porridge	To renew a discontinued sexual relationship
Warpaint Facial cosmetics	To destroy or bankrupt
Wash the baby's head	To drink intoxicants in celebration of a birth
Water closet	A lavatory with a flush mechanism
Water gardener	Someone who improperly releases confidential information to the media
Water of life (the)	Whiskey
Water stock	To render securities less valuable by constant dilution
Watering hole	A place licensed to sell intoxicants
Watermelon	An indication of pregnancy

Waterworks[2]	Tears
Wax	To remove unwanted hair from (a part of the body)
Weaker half (the)	Females
Weakness	A tendency towards self-indulgence
Wear the breeches	To be the dominant partner in a relationship between a man and a woman
Wear your heart upon your sleeve	To fail to conceal heterosexual longing
Wee drop	A drink of whiskey
Wee folk	The fairies
Wee (-wee)	To urinate
Weekend	Dishonestly to use a customer's money after the close of business on Friday
Weigh the thumb	Deliberately to overcharge
Weight watcher	A fat person
Welfare	State aid to the poor
Well built	Fat
Well-informed sources	The person involved
Wet nurse	A woman paid to suckle another's baby

Wet weekend	A period of menstruation
Wetness	Sweat
Whack	To kill. The common hitting imagery
Whiffed	Drunk
Whip	To steal
Whip the cat	To be drunk
White elephant	An unwanted or onerous possession
White feather	Cowardice
White girl	Heroin or cocaine
White flight	The loss of residential exclusivity. A phenomenon following the relocation of white householders from a locality following the ingress of less affluent non-whites
White knight	An industrial predator. In normal commercial jargon, a third party offering to save a company from an unwanted takeover. ...they are rightly sending 'white knights' packing when they show up with a flick knife up their sleeve
White-knuckler	A small aircraft on a scheduled service. Alluding to the anxious grip of the passengers on the arms of the seat, especially in bad weather. Various local carriers are called the white-knuckle line by their regular passengers

White marriage	A marriage in which the parties do not copulate The traditional virginal colour, so often seen inappropriately in the bridal gown, remains appropriate here
White meat	The breast of cooked poultry
White plague (the)	Pulmonary tuberculosis
White rabbit scut	Cowardice. The scut is the short white erect tail, the sign of the fleeing rabbit
White satin	Gin or vodka
White slave	A prostitute under the control of a pimp
White tail	A completed but unsold new aircraft
White top	A geriatric. A man so described may be bald, and a woman may have BLUE HAIR
White van man	A trader who does not observe the law
Whitewash	An attempt to hush up an embarrassing or shameful event
Wholesome	Not suffering from venereal disease
Windfall	A bribe
Window dressing	Falsely or fraudulently issuing figures or statements relating to a business
Winged	Wounded
Wire-pulling	The covert use of influence or pressure

With your maker	Dead
Without the highest IQ in the world	Slowwitted
Woman	A female viewed lustfully by a man
Woman friend	A mistress
Woman in a gilded cage	A mistress
Woman of the town	A prostitute
Women's rights	The claim to or enjoyment of economic and social conditions historically exclusive to or awarded in priority to men
Wooden box	A coffin
Word from our sponsor (a)	An advertisement on television would that it only one sells goods from
Work both sides of the street	To serve people with conflicting interests - to work a street was to attempt to sell goods from door to door
Work the streets	To be a prostitute from her public solicitation
Work to rule	To behave in a very calculated, to obstruct and cause loss
Work with writers	As an author to employ someone else to write the book

Workhouse	An institution for the homeless indigent
Working capital shortfall	An insolvency evasive circumlocution in a sphere of activity where a suggestion of failure must be avoided
Working dictionary	A mistress taken by an expatriate from the indigenous community
Workshop	A discussion group
Worship at the shrine of	To be unhealthily addicted to
Wrinkly	An old person
Write off	To kill or destroy
Written out of the script	Dismissed from employment. Literally, in the case of a television serial and figuratively of those not in show business
Wrong side of the blanket	An allusion to illegitimacy

Y

Yard bird	Convict
Yellow	Cowardly
Yellow page	Common or inferior. The implication is that those offering high quality goods or services do not have to advertise in the popular directory, yellow pages
Young	Not over 45 old

Z

Zero grazing. Intensive farming of cattle	The animals are confined to a barn or yard instead of being put out to pasture
Zipper	A male profligate
Zonked	Drunk or under the influence of illegal drugs